Dream Therapy for PTSD

Dream Therapy for PTSD

The Proven System for Ending Your Nightmares and Recovering from Trauma

Bruce Dow, MD

PRAEGER

AN IMPRINT OF ABC-CLIO, LLC
Santa Barbara, California • Denver, Colorado • Oxford, England

This book discusses treatments (including types of medication and mental health therapies), diagnostic tests for various symptoms and mental health disorders, and organizations. The authors have made every effort to present accurate and up-to-date information. However, the information in this book is not intended to recommend or endorse particular treatments or organizations, or substitute for the care or medical advice of a qualified health professional, or used to alter any medical therapy without a medical doctor's advice. Specific situations may require specific therapeutic approaches not included in this book. For those reasons, we recommend that readers follow the advice of qualified health care professionals directly involved in their care. Readers who suspect they may have specific medical problems should consult a physician about any suggestions made in this book.

Library of Congress Cataloging-in-Publication Data

Dow, Bruce (Psychiatrist)
Dream therapy for PTSD : the proven system for ending your nightmares and recovering from trauma / Bruce Dow, MD.
pages cm
Includes bibliographical references and index.
ISBN 978-1-4408-3740-1 (alk. paper)—ISBN 978-1-4408-3741-8 (ebook) 1. Post-traumatic stress disorder—Treatment. 2. Dreams—Therapeutic use. 3. Nightmares. I. Title.
RC552.P67D69 2015
616.85′2106—dc23 2014041802

ISBN: 978-1-4408-3740-1
EISBN: 978-1-4408-3741-8

19 18 17 16 15 1 2 3 4 5

This book is also available on the World Wide Web as an eBook.
Visit www.abc-clio.com for details.

Praeger
An Imprint of ABC-CLIO, LLC

ABC-CLIO, LLC
130 Cremona Drive, P.O. Box 1911
Santa Barbara, California 93116-1911

This book is printed on acid-free paper ∞

Manufactured in the United States of America

To the Dream Group veterans who started me on this project

Contents

There are those that look at things the way they are, and ask why? I dream of things that never were, and ask why not?

Robert F. Kennedy

Acknowledgments

Thanks to my book coach, Lisa Tener, who helped me develop my voice; to fellow writing students Anne Burnett, Martha Rhodes, and Norah Hall for valuable feedback during writing sessions with Lisa; and to Julie Silver and the Harvard Writers Conference for teaching me about medical nonfiction writing and introducing me to Lisa. Thanks to Debbie Carvalko, Bridget Austiguy-Preschel at ABC-CLIO, Praeger Press, and Nicholle Lutz at BookComp, Inc., who helped me convert the manuscript into a book. Thanks to my agent Bob DiForio.

Thanks to my patients for sharing their stories so that other people suffering from PTSD might benefit from their experiences. Thanks to Doug Bintliff for listening to my telling of the stories during mountain walks, and to my brothers, Dave Dow and Bill Dow, for reading the manuscript and giving me helpful comments.

Thanks to Rusty Shelton and his group for website development, Sara Jane Lapp for videos, Stephen DeFronzo for portrait photography. Thanks to Ken Duckworth, for his internet radio interview with me on "Meet the Doctor"; and to Michele Rosenthal for having me on her internet radio show, "Your Life After Trauma," three times, for valuable on-air interactions with PTSD survivors.

Thanks to Jim Maguire for discussions regarding extinction, memory, and trauma; and to the South-Eastern Massachusetts Psychiatric Society (SEMPS) for inviting me to present case histories from the book for discussions of treatment strategies.

And, most importantly, thanks to my partner, Rae Edelson, for her support and encouragement during all phases of the development and publication of this book.

ONE

Rescript Your Dreams and Recover from PTSD

I am a psychiatrist with a special interest in posttraumatic stress disorder (PTSD). In the early 1990s while working with Vietnam veterans at the San Diego VA hospital, I was amazed to see that a particular type of therapy involving nightmare revision could get rid of posttraumatic nightmares that had been occurring several times per week over a period of 25 years or more (since the Vietnam War). Once the nightmares stopped, patients recovered from their PTSD, not immediately, but within a few months to a few years.[1]

For several decades now, in conjunction with prescription writing as a practicing psychopharmacologist, I have helped patients change their posttraumatic nightmares into dreams. People have repeatedly asked me for a book about nightmare revision in the treatment of PTSD. In *Dream Therapy for PTSD* I share my experiences and the experiences of my patients, in hopes that others with nightmares and PTSD may be liberated from recurrent nightmares, and lose their PTSD in the process.

In my practice, when people's dreams change on their own and progress from session to session, I provide support and encouragement, pointing out correlations between changes in their lives and changes in their dreams. I also call attention to practical suggestions that may be hinted at or suggested by a particular dream. Whenever people's dreams seem to be stuck in a recurrent pattern, I introduce the specific methodology of dream revision, encouraging the dreamer to work at changing (and eliminating) his or her recurrent nightmare.

Dream Therapy for PTSD documents instances in which people were able to rid themselves of nightmares that had lasted months to years. Along with relief from nightmares came relief from the accompanying emotions of anxiety, frustration, sadness, anger, hopelessness, helplessness, and worthlessness. PTSD symptoms gradually disappeared, and people found themselves able to return to work, sometimes after years of chronic disability.

The dream revision method works for nightmares from all types of trauma, whether in everyday life or military combat. Because of the nature of my particular psychiatric practice, most of the traumas reported here were work related for my clients. Others have shown dream revision techniques to be effective in posttraumatic nightmares associated with interpersonal violence (rape, robbery, molestation) and vehicular accidents.[2]

MARISA: TRAUMA FROM WITNESSING

Marisa was a 34-year-old married Hispanic woman with two young children when she came to see me in 2002. She arrived late, saying she got confused about the directions to my office. She was restless and fidgety, uneasy about being there, clearly unaccustomed to seeing a psychiatrist.

Marisa worked as recreation manager of a large San Diego resort hotel. Just two weeks earlier—while vacuuming the water at the hotel's outdoor swimming pool—she was startled by a huge noise and the sound of breaking glass. Just a few feet from where Marisa stood, she saw a woman's body lying at the pool's edge. The woman was still alive, moaning, with her eyes bulging out, and her internal organs protruding through open and visible skin wounds. Marisa realized that the woman had fallen from as many as 15 stories up above the pool patio.

Marisa wanted to run and call 911, but felt as if she couldn't move. Pool attendants and trainers came over and tried to help. There were so many people around. Marisa said, "It felt like forever until the ambulance came." She later learned that the woman had jumped off a balcony 12 floors above, and had died in the ambulance on the way to the hospital.

Marisa continued to work after the commotion settled down. In fact, she worked 17 hours, from 5 a.m. to 10 p.m. When she had a moment to herself in the pump room, she cried, but then stopped herself. She felt she had to keep working; it was her duty to her employer.

She returned home to find her husband asleep. She didn't wake him, knowing he had to get up early for work in the morning, and she didn't want to disturb him. Unable to sleep herself, she went into the bathroom and cried. All night long she experienced flashbacks about the scene at work, imagining the falling body, and remembering the sound of the impact, the breaking glass, the appearance of the woman, her moaning sounds.

The next day she went to work late. At work she felt as if her head might explode. The muscles in the back of her neck were tight. She felt nauseated and vomited. She couldn't concentrate, and after a few miserable hours, she returned home. That night she had nightmares about her children drowning.

The next day—two days after the incident—she called the hotel's 800 number to get help. She was seen by their medical director, who prescribed Xanax for anxiety, placed her on medical disability leave, and made arrangements for her to see a psychiatrist.

She came to my office two weeks after the incident. "I'm having nightmares about the woman who jumped," she said, "and about my mother's death when I was 17. Remembering what happened at the hotel makes me nervous, and I start shaking." She shook visibly as she shared the details with me.

Marisa had grown up in Mexico, the second youngest of eight children. Her parents separated when she was just a few months old, and she and several of her siblings moved to another city with their mother until Marisa turned 13. Her mother worked long hours in a restaurant, leaving little or no time for her children. An older sister raised Marisa and ran the household. "In Mexico," Marisa told me, "they don't talk to you; they hit you." When Marisa turned 13, her sister decided that Marisa should move to San Diego to live with their brother.

Marisa cleaned houses in San Diego for a number of years. She met her husband about 10 years before the hotel incident. They had two daughters—ages eight and three—at the time of the incident. Marisa's husband worked as a cook and gardener at a local university; Marisa had worked at the hotel for five years.

Marisa's mother died in her mid-fifties of a heart problem following hernia surgery in Mexico while Marisa was visiting. Marisa rode with her mother in the ambulance to the hospital. The ambulance driver asked Marisa to hold two babies, which prevented her from holding her mother's hand. Her mother never woke up after the surgery.

Seeing the woman lying unconscious and moaning at the hotel's outdoor swimming pool reminded Marisa of her mother's death after hernia surgery 17 years earlier. Nightmares and flashbacks of the two situations merged in Marisa's mind.

When I first saw Marisa, I diagnosed "acute stress disorder." Since the incident had occurred less than 30 days earlier, it was technically too soon to make the diagnosis of posttraumatic stress disorder (PTSD).[3] I elected to continue her Xanax, and added an antidepressant for anxiety and insomnia, and to ward off PTSD and depression. Marisa reported three recurrent dreams:

Dream 1: Killing Myself and My Kids

I kill my kids (shooting with a gun or drowning); then kill myself (the same way I kill my kids).

Dreams 2 and 3: My Kids are Drowning

My kids are drowning and I can't save them. There is so much dark water. (I have a different dream about each daughter.) In the dream about my older daughter, I'm trying to reach out to her. In the dream about my younger daughter, I'm swimming underwater to get to her, but I can't hold my breath long enough. I'm trying to wake up. I'm trying to get my husband to wake me up.

I decided to try dream revision therapy with Dreams 2 and 3. Marissa and I discussed possible revisions, and came up with the following ideas: 1) get a pole hook (from the swimming pool at the hotel where she works); reach out to her older daughter; and have her grab onto it; 2) get a lifeguard to rescue her younger daughter. We reviewed the revisions until I felt sure that Marisa would remember them. I asked her to share her dreams, both the original and revised versions, with a trusted person: her husband, another family member, or a close friend.

When I spoke with her by phone several weeks later, Marisa indicated she had rehearsed the dream revisions as advised. She said the lifeguard assistance had worked; the nightmare about her younger daughter was gone. However, the revision involving Marisa getting a pole hook from the swimming pool had not worked; she still had the nightmare about her older daughter drowning. I advised her to provide a "dream" lifeguard to assist her older daughter as well. She liked this idea and agreed to give it a try.

At our next session, about a month after the initial dream revision session, Marisa told me she had rehearsed the dream image of providing lifeguard assistance for her older daughter, and all three nightmares had now stopped. She felt much better, and had returned to her old job as recreation manager. While it was difficult at first, she made the adjustment. She still experienced occasional flashbacks, was easily startled, and would get upset when reminded of the incident, indicating she was experiencing PTSD, but at only at a mild-to-moderate level.

Within several months, she reported being essentially fully recovered. She experienced no further nightmares or flashbacks, her startle response was gone, and she felt less agitated by reminders of the swimming pool incident. She returned to work full time and no longer felt the need to come to see me.

TOM: TRAUMA FROM KILLING

When I first saw Tom, in December 1995, I could hardly believe my eyes. I wondered if this enormous man—six feet five inches tall, 340 pounds, only slightly overweight for his size—might have been a lineman for the San Diego Chargers. Not a current lineman—he was 46 years old—but maybe a former one. He told me he was a linebacker in college, and had considered playing pro football, but joined the Army instead.

Tom served in Vietnam from 1968 to 1970—the peak of the war. He saw extensive combat as an airborne ranger—parachuting from airplanes—and a platoon leader in the infantry. He fought at Hamburger Hill, one of the bloodiest battles of the war. Tom was wounded in the hip and ankle in Vietnam and now walked with implanted prostheses in both legs.

Before coming to see me, Tom worked for several years on the staff of Vietnam Veterans of San Diego (VVSD), a program that provided housing and job training for Vietnam Veterans. He was a generous and caring man—a gentle giant.

Tom lived in the San Diego suburbs with his second wife, who was younger than he was and worked as a 911 operator and police dispatcher. They were raising three children—their own four-year-old daughter, and Tom's teenage son and daughter from his first marriage. Tom was on total and permanent disability for his war injuries, including the psychological ones. He stayed home and managed the household while his wife worked.

Tom was troubled by a recurrent nightmare that recalled an actual wartime experience, when he had shot and then suffocated a Vietnamese boy in an effort to stop him from screaming. Tom was 19 at the time. Ever since the incident 27 years earlier,—Tom endured this nightmare once or twice every week. Whenever he had the nightmare, he got up and checked the perimeter around his house to make sure there were no enemy soldiers lurking in the bushes outside.

Initially Tom had self-medicated himself with illegal drugs, whatever he could get his hands on, heroin, cocaine, marijuana, crystal meth, Demerol, morphine. He was an IV junkie for two years back in the 1970s. He stole his mother's morphine when she was dying of cancer in the early 1980s.

His first wife had left him eight years earlier because of his drug use. He became sober at that time, in order to take care of the two children she left with him. For the past eight years he had been active in Alcoholics Anonymous (AA), still attended meetings four times per week, and was now on the AA central phone list to field calls from people in crisis. He met his second wife six years before his first meeting with me.

The PTSD significantly disabled Tom. He experienced nightmares, flashbacks, startle reactions, unwanted memories, and bouts of anger. He stayed at home because he felt safe there. Even at home, he was often irritable, verbally abusive to family members, and afraid he might lose control, though, so far, was never physically violent. I treated him with supportive therapy, dream revision therapy, and medication for PTSD and depression.

Tom and I worked together on two recurrent dreams.

Dream 1: Suffocated Boy

A Vietnamese boy, age nine, comes out of the bushes and surprises my six-man surveillance patrol team. I shoot him, and then suffocate him accidentally while trying to stop him from screaming.

Tom told me this dream at our first session. The dream made him feel guilty, sad, and angry, and kept him awake whenever he had it. The next day he would feel terrible all day long. He thought about his own children and imagined how the parents of that nine-year-old Vietnamese boy must have felt to lose their child.

Doing dream revision therapy on a dream that repeats a real situation—as with Tom's dream—is more challenging than working with dreams like Marisa's which create fictional situations. Dreamers sometimes object that they can't change a situation that actually occurred. I tell them, as I told Tom, that the event occurred in the past—the distant past in Tom's case—and is now just a video recording playing over and over in their head like a "broken record" or a scratched DVD.

The basic idea in changing a dream like Tom's is to respect the dream's integrity while changing its outcome. The change should be as minor as possible, but have a major impact. This takes practice, but becomes easier once you learn how to do it. A major goal of *Dream Therapy for PTSD* is to teach you the techniques of dream revision by seeing how my patients and I use them with real dreams.

Tom and I considered a few options. We could have the boy just stay at home and not appear, but that would not allow the dream to get started.

The boy could be there at the dream scene, but stay in the bushes. How would we know he was there? Tom could shoot and miss the boy, but then the boy might make a lot of noise running away and could alert others. The solution Tom and I came up with was to change the boy into a Viet Cong (enemy soldier), that is, not just a boy but a young combatant. Killing an enemy combatant (instead of a boy) could relieve Tom of much of the guilt he had been feeling.

I told Tom to go home and rehearse the revised dream.

- Write it down to make it real.
- Tell a veteran friend the new dream.
- Get the new dream solidly implanted in his mind.
- Go to sleep (that night and each night until our next appointment) and see what happens.

I saw Tom 2 weeks later and the nightmare had not yet returned. Over the next 12 years I worked with Tom (I was authorized to see him monthly for medication management) the nightmare never returned. His nightmare of 27 years was finally gone for good. Within a few months of our single and successful dream revision session Tom began to show clear signs of improvement. His guilt, sadness, and anger decreased. He felt more open to life, more able to enjoy his family and friends. However, Tom was not yet completely healed. He had another recurrent dream about a Vietnamese boy.

Dream 2: Popsicle Boy

A young Vietnamese boy (age six or seven) is selling popsicles out of an ammo canister. Explosion of the canister kills two of my buddies. I shoot the boy with my M16 rifle.

Tom shared Dream 2 with me after we had been meeting for about six months. This dream involved a different boy and a different actual incident from Vietnam. It seemed almost like a recurrence of Dream 1, but was a distinctly different dream. Perhaps our solution for Dream 1 had brought that dream back in a modified form.

This time we made a different change. We took the explosion and all killing out of the dream. The boy passes out popsicles and then just goes away with his backpack and canister. There is no explosion. The boy smiles and waves as he leaves. He is not an enemy. Tom smiles back and waves his own greeting.

I told Tom to focus on imagining the smiling, waving boy rather than the explosion. I also reminded him to write down the revised version and share it with other veterans, to make it more real. Generally, veterans prefer not to discuss combat experiences with family members, but with other veterans who were in the combat zone and understand the situation better.

Tom rehearsed the revised dream, successfully preventing the recurrence of Dream 2 for a year. At the end of the year, while Tom was vacationing in Hawaii with friends, playing golf in terrain reminiscent of Vietnam, a helicopter flew just above his golf party, making the whirring chop-chop sound that he remembered from Vietnam. He immediately experienced a flashback to the popsicle incident, and that night had the popsicle nightmare again. Tom used the same dream revision we had worked on a year earlier, and the nightmare stopped again without much difficulty. As he developed skill in dream revision, he could feel his confidence improving.

Over the next 10 years in our monthly sessions, Tom mentioned having occasional nightmares about Vietnam experiences, especially in relation to anniversary dates that came along each year, but he controlled the nightmares, using the dream revision technique he had learned.

About a year before our first meeting in 1995, Tom had developed diabetes, for which he got both insulin injections and pills. Later he managed with pills alone. In 2003 he developed an infection in his left foot, which led to osteomyelitis (bone infection) and eventually a below-the-knee (BK) amputation of his left leg. The VA rehab program made him a special prosthesis so he could continue to play golf. A few years later he developed an infection in his right foot, which again led to osteomyelitis, and in 2005 his right leg had to be amputated below the knee as well.

After his recovery from the two amputations, it was very moving for me to see Tom come into my office in shorts with his two prostheses showing, and his four-year-old grandson in tow. He brought his grandson into my office and they played together on the floor while Tom and I conducted our medication management/supportive therapy session. Tom was in fairly good spirits about his prostheses. He could play golf on them, utilizing special swivel joints at the ankles.

Tom volunteered his services to help returning Iraq War veterans who had lost one or more limbs. He developed a strategy for meeting young veterans receiving treatment in the rehab hospital. Tom, with his large imposing frame, arrived at the hospital walking normally and dressed casually in a short-sleeve shirt and long pants. He walked up to a group of disabled veterans from the war in Iraq, and introduced himself as Tom, retired Vietnam War veteran, airborne ranger, and infantry platoon leader. The vets then introduced themselves, and Tom asked them about their experiences in Iraq. After the conversation had been going a while, Tom found an excuse to lift his two pantlegs and reveal his prostheses to his new young friends.

Tom inspired me, and I imagine he inspired the young disabled Iraq War veterans as well. He had found a way to derive meaning from his own war experiences and their aftermath. He not only revised his dreams, but then accepted and revised himself.

MY BACKGROUND IN PTSD AND DREAMING

I first became interested in posttraumatic stress disorder (PTSD) during my psychiatry residency training in the early 1990s—in the context of the first Gulf War—when many Vietnam War veterans appeared in clinics for treatment of their PTSD symptoms, which were triggered by television news reports and newspaper accounts of the Gulf War. I worked as a psychiatry resident and psychopharmacology fellow at the University of California, San Diego (UCSD). My colleagues and I conducted research studies on the sleep and dreams of Vietnam veterans with PTSD,[4] and I began collecting dreams from the PTSD patients I treated in the university clinic at the VA hospital.

Prior to my psychiatric residency I had been a vision researcher and professor (in the Physiology Department) at the State University of New York (SUNY) Buffalo, and before that a vision researcher at the National Institutes of Health (NIH) in Bethesda, MD. Over more than 20 years as a vision researcher I published many articles on the visual functioning of the brain. My special interest was in color vision.[5]

Within psychiatry, I chose the field of PTSD because it is both visual and emotional. I have an ongoing interest in the "mapping" of colors and emotions in the brain. PTSD involves emotional memories which fail to get properly stored in the brain. I am interested in where and how emotional memories are stored. Rescripting nightmares and helping people recover from PTSD may provide answers to such questions.

While prescribing psychotropic medications to my patients, I ask about their dreams. If a patient has a recurrent nightmare, I offer to help them get rid of it through dream revision. Typically, I continue the medications if they are helpful, and do dream revision as an adjunct treatment. When dream revision works, it goes right to the site of the traumatic injury in the brain, like a magic bullet. In contrast, the medications seem to act only around the edges of the trauma. Later in the book we will look more closely at brain mechanisms of posttraumatic stress disorder, in hopes of understanding how dream revision may actually work.

POSTTRAUMATIC STRESS DISORDER

Posttraumatic stress disorder (PTSD) became an official psychiatric diagnosis in the United States in 1980, when many returning veterans from the Vietnam War reported suffering from a particular cluster of symptoms, including nightmares, flashbacks, and intrusive memories of traumatic combat experiences.[6]

The condition is by no means a new one. Homer described symptoms of PTSD 2,800 years ago in his accounts of the Trojan War and its aftermath in *The Iliad* and *The Odyssey*.[7] PTSD, or something akin to it, was recognized in World War I and II and referred to as "soldier's heart," "battle fatigue," "combat neurosis," or "traumatic neurosis."[8]

Our present-day understanding of PTSD is summarized in the current version of the Diagnostic and Statistical Manual of Mental Disorders (DSM-IV TR, 2000).[9] A patient is considered to have PTSD when he or she has 1) experienced, witnessed, or been confronted with a life-threatening event, and 2) has had a response involving intense fear, helplessness, or horror. Symptoms of reexperiencing (memories, dreams, flashbacks), avoidance (memory loss, detachment, numbing), and arousal (anger, vigilance, startle) also need to be present. The disturbance must last more than a month and must cause significant behavioral disability. Posttraumatic stress lasting less than a month is called "acute stress disorder." In the case of Marisa, presented earlier, symptoms might have lasted many months (even years) if she had not gotten therapy so soon after her traumatic injury. Since Marisa's symptoms persisted for several months after her initial injury, she did technically progress to PTSD, though in a reduced form.

Recent studies indicate that nightmares are a crucial component of PTSD.[10] Eliminating nightmares is a major first step toward eliminating PTSD. If you suffer from nightmares and PTSD, this book can help you be free, not only of nightmares, but of PTSD as well. The recovery process is likely to be quicker (days to weeks) with PTSD of recent onset (like Marisa's), but even with PTSD of many years' duration (as in Tom's case) you have a significant chance of recovering (in weeks to months) if you work at eliminating your nightmares, using the techniques described in this book.

OTHER TYPES OF THERAPY FOR PTSD

Traditional psychoanalysis was not designed to address PTSD. According to Freud's original theory, dreaming is a mechanism for fulfilling unconscious (and sometimes forbidden) wishes while we sleep.[11] This certainly cannot be true for posttraumatic dreams, which are anything but wish fulfilling. Posttraumatic dreams are frightening, even sometimes terrifying, and lead PTSD sufferers to avoid the experiences of everyday life, out of fear that something unexpected (a sight, sound, smell, taste, or touch) might trigger a flashback or nightmare.[12]

In addition to dream revision, there are two other types of modern psychotherapy that address PTSD symptoms with some success—prolonged exposure (PE) therapy, introduced by Edna Foa and her colleagues,[13] and eye movement desensitization and reprocessing (EMDR), introduced by Francine Shapiro and her colleagues.[14] Both methods involve exposure to the trauma, though the details of the exposure are different.

An advantage of dream revision over these other two methods is that dreams are often symbolic, allowing a trauma to be addressed indirectly (within the symbolism, as in Marisa's dreams), rather than face-to-face. This can be less frightening and less threatening, for both patient and therapist.

NIGHTMARE REVISION AND PTSD

Dream revision techniques have been in use for centuries in the form of fairy tales, myths, and legends in many cultures of the world, which help both children and adults conquer their fears of dream monsters, by creating plots in which the initial victims emerge victorious after a variety of dangers are overcome. Bruno Bettelheim, a Viennese psychoanalyst who survived two concentration camps—Dachau and Buchenwald—described the meaning and importance of fairy tales in his book, *The Uses of Enchantment* (1976).

If you suffer from posttraumatic stress disorder (PTSD), getting rid of your nightmare can be therapeutic for your PTSD itself. The nightmare is a kind of spell like the one Sleeping Beauty is put under by the wicked witch. Dream revision breaks the spell, and frees you to go on with your life.

You may be able to learn how to do dream revision simply by reading this book, which contains many examples of dream revisions that succeeded in getting rid of nightmares. The process may be easier if your nightmare is symbolic or metaphorical, and you can recognize that it relates to your trauma. A therapist might be needed to help you decipher the metaphor, but many people learn this readily, as in the case of Marisa, and in other examples scattered through the book. Marisa understood that her dreams were not really about her children drowning, but about the woman dying in front of her.

If your dream is not metaphorical, but actually repeats the trauma—as in Tom's two dreams—then you need to think of it as a video recording from the past, playing over and over in your head, or a derailed train with its wheels still spinning. Whatever image works best for you, the goal is to change the nightmare—in some seemingly minor but critical way—into a dream, as Tom and I did with his two dreams.

As mentioned earlier, it is important in doing this to respect and validate the dream's integrity and its grounding in historical events. With successful dream revision, the dreaming mechanisms of the brain are somehow jump-started and normal dreaming takes over. The video progresses to a new scene; the train moves forward. Not only does normal dreaming resume, but one's life resumes as well.

Once you have learned how to change one nightmare—either on your own or with a therapist—you can use the method to get rid of other nightmares as they arise.

FOUR STEPS IN DREAM REVISION

- Create a narrative version of the dream.
- Revise the narrative to provide a happy ending.
- Rehearse the revised version of the dream.
- Go to sleep and see what happens.

TIPS FOR DREAM REVISION FROM CHAPTER 1

1. If a dream doesn't change or go away after the first revision attempt, as in Marisa's Dream 2 (My Kids Are Drowning), keep trying until you find a solution that works.
2. Sometimes a revised recurrent dream will return, as in Tom's Dream 2 (Popsicle Boy). A different revision may be called for, which seemed to work here, as Tom's dreams about killing Vietnamese boys did not return after we revised his second recurrent dream.

TWO

The Dream Team: Group Therapy for Combat Nightmares

As mentioned, I became interested in PTSD in the early 1990s during my psychiatric residency and fellowship training at the University of California, San Diego (UCSD), from 1991 to 1994. The first Iraq (Persian Gulf) War had begun in August 1990, with the invasion of Kuwait by Iraqi troops under the command of military dictator, Saddam Hussein. A coalition force of 34 nations was organized through the United Nations to oppose the Iraqi invasion. The coalition's operations began in January 1991, with an aerial bombardment followed by a ground assault. The ground campaign lasted only 100 hours (four days). At that point Iraqi forces had been driven out of Kuwait, and U.S. president George H.W. Bush declared a cease-fire without attempting to occupy Baghdad or remove Saddam Hussein from power.

As I began working with patients at the San Diego VA Medical Center, I noticed that many of them, primarily Vietnam War veterans, had symptoms of PTSD. In many cases their PTSD had not been clearly diagnosed and was not being treated. In some cases it was being masked by substance abuse.

The first Gulf War, broadcast on all the network news programs (CBS, NBC, ABC) and with continuous coverage on the Cable News Network (CNN), was in everyone's living room every day. Scenes of active military combat in the Persian Gulf triggered flashbacks and nightmares for many Vietnam veterans and brought them into outpatient clinics and inpatient units with reactivated PTSD. Standard antidepressant and antianxiety medications reduced PTSD symptoms somewhat, but patients remained vulnerable to triggers. Many stayed isolated in their rooms or retreated to cabins in the woods to avoid the nearly ubiquitous triggers.

It became clear to many of us that in order to treat PTSD effectively one needed to address the trauma itself. However, the mere prospect of doing this was frightening to Vietnam veterans. By this time, in the early 1990s, the Vietnam War (which peaked in the late 1960s and ended in the early 1970s) had been over for nearly 20 years. The first Gulf War was already causing Vietnam veterans to relive Vietnam in their flashbacks and nightmares. They had no interest in reliving the Vietnam War with civilian therapists like myself who had not even been to Vietnam, much less seen combat there.

At the San Diego VA Medical Center we were in the process of setting up therapy groups for our PTSD program, which included an outpatient clinic and a small inpatient unit. I was doing sleep research with PTSD patients and serving as acting director of the inpatient PTSD program.[1] I thought it would be interesting to run a therapy group dealing with nightmares in PTSD patients. There were already indications in the psychiatric literature that PTSD might be a sleep disorder.[2]

A paper by Brockway (1987) indicated that combat nightmares could be "detoxified" in a group treatment setting. The treatment had been conducted at the Phoenix VA Medical Center. After reading the paper I called the Phoenix VA Medical Center and spoke with the director of their "Combat Stress Program," Jose Amado, MD, who updated me on the current status of their PTSD dream group. We developed our San Diego VA "Dream Team" program following the Phoenix model. Our program ran once a week for 32 sessions, from November 1993 to July 1994.

Typically we had between 5 and 10 patients per group plus myself and several staff members (usually a psychiatric nurse and a medical student). Each one-hour session was devoted to a single patient selected by the staff from people who indicated they would be willing to provide a dream. We encouraged group participants to come prepared to present a dream, including a written dream text, if possible, to share with the group.

While the patient presented his dream to the group, a staff member wrote the dream text on a whiteboard. A designated secretary (usually a patient) copied the dream text, along with group commentary, into a notebook as a permanent record.

Once the dream text was on the whiteboard for all to see, the group members asked questions of the dreamer. How often had he had this dream? When was the first time, the last time? Had the dream changed at all over the years, or was it always the same? Subjects were asked to provide recurrent dreams, which they had typically been having for years, often with some variation in details from one recurrence to the next. Some subjects maintained that their recurrent dream was always exactly the same.

The dreamer was asked to recall any triggers that could bring on the dream. Examples might be a helicopter flying overhead, the smell of Vietnamese food coming from a restaurant, Fourth of July fireworks, red (blood) and green (khaki) Christmas decorations, the sound of empty Coke cans rattling against each other (attached to barbed wire around campsites to warn of Viet Cong approaching), the feel and smell of a rainy day (triple canopy rainforest setting in Vietnam). Discussing triggers in this way helped everyone, including the dreamer, become more aware of the role of triggers in provoking nightmares. Understanding one's triggers provides an increase in one's sense of control. One can then avoid avoidable triggers and be better prepared to deal with unavoidable triggers when they occur.

Next, the dreamer was asked to describe specific emotions or feelings that the dream aroused in him. Examples might be fear, anger, shame, guilt, frustration, and sadness. This helped all group members to get in better touch with their own feelings. Patients with PTSD have a high incidence of "alexithymia," or difficulty putting a name to their emotions.[3] Discussing feelings helped to reduce alexithymia in group members. Another reason to have the dreamer share his emotions was for the group to get ideas as to what sort of dream revision might be most helpful. If the dreamer felt scared or helpless, assistance might be provided in the form of reinforcements. If the dreamer felt ashamed or guilty, we might look for a way to boost his confidence or pride.

The group then engaged in a brainstorming process, analyzing the dream, trying to understand its surface meaning as well as possible hidden (metaphorical) meanings. We sought to avoid speculation, while not being absolutely limited to the literal details.

Group members were asked to propose changes to the dream. All suggestions were put on the whiteboard in the form of a list. The dreamer was asked to select the change that he preferred, combining several changes if he so chose. I noticed (as did other participants) that a successful dream revision was often accompanied by a smile on the dreamer's face. When we saw that smile, we felt we had achieved a good revision.

The dreamer was then instructed to rehearse the revision repeatedly over the next week, until the group would meet again, writing down the revised text if he could, and then to report back to us regarding any subsequent changes in his dream.

An important component of the dream revision group, I later discovered, was the support and encouragement that was provided after the session, from individual group members talking among themselves and from support staff on the inpatient unit. Without such assistance from support staff, when I have tried dream revision groups in my private office as the sole therapist with a group of PTSD patients (whether veterans or civilians), the sessions have proved too intense and unsettling. People had difficulty returning home without emotional support. Some people in such an office setting became suicidal, occasionally to the extent of requiring hospital admission. In my experience, then, dream revision group therapy for recurrent nightmares in PTSD patients typically requires an inpatient or at least a hospital setting.

At this point it is instructive to review some data from our inpatient dream revision group. A total of 26 patients provided dreams for 32 sessions in all, with 6 patients providing dreams for 2 sessions, and 1 patient providing dreams for 3 sessions. We devoted the initial portion of each session to follow-up reports from previous sessions. We tried to keep the follow-up reports as brief as possible, so as not to reduce the time for the current dream revision session. Since many dreams did change, the reports amounted to endorsements of the method, and provided a positive background with which to begin each new session.

VETERANS' DREAMS

Table 2.1 summarizes the overall data, the date of the dream revision session, the dream title, and follow-up results. To examine the dream revision process in detail, we will focus on several individual dreams.

Dream 2: 11/16/93 Escape from Pumpkin Hill

Starts out, I see from the waist down, boots and rifle. It's dark, but you can see. I never see the top. I try to put myself there, but it erases. Walking along and you see small vines; then they get larger. Then I see pumpkins in clusters, some small and then they get larger. Then the pumpkins smile and we shoot them. Just before you pull the trigger there is a face on them. It becomes a game, then, to shoot them before the face appears. Endless fields of pumpkins. There's a hill, but we can't get up because it's too slick. Keep trying, but can't get up. Don't look back at the pumpkins. Spend the night attempting to go up, and slipping back. Always afraid that I missed one. If I missed one, it will get me. The voice says "You've done this before, you can do it again." Faces are Vietnamese. Most are faces seen in search and destroy in villages.

Table 2.1 VA Dream Revision Group

#	Date	Id	Dream Title	Outcome
1	11/02/93	jg	Stony's rockpile	not known
2	11/16/93	gy	escape from Pumpkin Hill	less often
3	11/26/93	pg	the devil and mister Pete	gone
4	12/03/93	dp	flip-flop white rabbit	gone
5	12/10/93	bw	freedom ride	changed
6	12/17/93	be	Diane & the seven dwarfs	gone
7	12/21/93	eb	thanks from the past	gone
8	01/04/94	em	freedom waters; dead fucker	gone
9	01/14/94	bs	exit laughing	less often
10	01/21/94	lm	getting even	gone
11	01/26/94	el	clearing of mind	unchanged
12	02/02/94	eg	war and peace	gone
13	02/09/94	jr	Mary Ann	gone+
14	02/15/94	bh	skeleton & water buffalo	less often
15	02/23/94	mc	this is only a drill	worse
16	03/02/94	rz	put Ringo back together	changed
17	03/16/94	co	Andre's reality	gone+
18	03/23/94	jb	corpsman in training	changed
19	03/30/94	gd	doc saves a life	gone+
20	04/06/94	jm	surviving day two	gone+
21	04/13/94	bp	freedom bird	less often
22	04/20/94	jl	thank you doc	unchanged
23	04/27/94	me	near hit	less often
24	05/04/94	bp	night to day	less often
25	05/11/94	gd	doc's reward	gone+
26	05/18/94	ae	the great escape	gone
27	05/25/94	co	guardian angel Paul	gone+
28	06/01/94	jb	training exercises	not known
29	06/08/94	gd	life prospers	gone+
30	06/22/94	bc	the extraction	less often
31	07/12/94	jr	escape and evasion	gone+
32	07/26/94	js	nomad	not known

+ long-term follow-up

During the discussion, the dreamer reported that the dream was recurrent on a regular basis. Many things could bring it on, including stress, anger, and fatigue. Our group interpretation was that the pumpkins were Vietnamese people in villages. The slipping was the frustration he and other American soldiers felt.

Several changes to the dream were proposed:

1) Change the pumpkins to watermelons.
2) Look back at the pumpkins.
3) Say no to the voice.
4) Get rid of the rifle (to have two free hands).
5) Fight back; protect yourself.
6) Dig foothold steps in the hill, and get to the top; once over the hill, it's OK.

The dreamer chose option 6. He explained that his main concern in the dream was to get better footing so he could make it to the top of the hill. That was all he really needed.

Dream 7: 12/21/93 Thanks from the Past

On the Freedom Bird jet (plane returning soldiers from Vietnam to the United States). The plane stands on its tail, takes off, goes straight up, and cracks open. We all fall out. We land back in the jungle. I'm the only one not hurt. Everybody else's body parts are lying around, missing heads, arms, legs. I pick up body parts, try to reassemble guys. I can't get the right parts on the right bodies. I reach for my aid bag. It's not there. The heads start yelling at me, "do it right." I try and can't get it done. They all start chasing me. I know if they catch me, they'll take my head or disassemble me. I'm running through the jungle scared as hell. Just before they catch me I wake up.

Suggested changes:

1) Get the body parts right. Guys say "thank you, you did a good job."
2) Automobile instead of Freedom Bird (avoids crash).
3) Escorting the bodies back home on a cruise ship, with entertainment, topless dancing. When the ship reaches home, the families of the dead are there to thank him for helping them.

The dreamer assembled the following revised dream from the above suggestions provided by other Dream Team members:

"I put all the body parts into the correct bags for transport back home. I accompany the body bags on a C-140 Air Force transport plane. The plane returns home to Travis Air Force Base in California. Family members of the deceased are there to meet the plane and thank me for my help. I feel my work is completed."

The Dream Team also gave the dreamer some advice for the future. They suggested he go to the Vietnam Memorial Wall in Washington, D.C., with a friend, and that he also go see the miniature traveling version of the D.C. Wall when it came to San Diego. They told him to feel good about himself, that he had done the best he could.

Dream 13: 02/09/94 Mary Ann

At Mary Ann. Early in the a.m. (4:30). Fire base got hit with over a hundred rockets. Communication got hit. How I woke up I have no idea. A dead hit. Everybody in the bunker is blown to pieces. Zappers are coming through the wire with satchel charges. They are camouflaged, with monster faces, horror movie faces. I am running back and forth, looking for my friend, John. All I can find is his head. I go into a rage. I sleep with a Bowie knife. Every zapper that passes by me, I cut his throat. By the time the light comes, we get some helicopter gunships. They get rid of the Viet Cong. There are bodies all over the place. Over 800 pieces of bodies lying all over the place. It gets hard. My mind goes blank. I wake up in a hospital in Chu Ly. Time blanks out on me. There are a lot of Vietnamese bodies too. There is a strong odor from the bodies. It is raining. All my family, my brothers, my buddies are lying there. My friend, John, just his head is lying there. Everything finishes at about 6:30 a.m.

Suggested changes:

1) VC spies on our side warn of the attack, and we evacuate the bunkers.
2) We prestrike against their rockets (air strikes) with rockets and napalm.
3) We bomb specific areas on the Ho Chi Minh trail, using propeller planes.
4) We change the attack into a training exercise with live ammo.

5) We level Hanoi, make it into a parking lot with bombs, nuclear weapons.
6) I wake up; John is in the next bunk.

The dreamer constructed the following revised dream from the above suggestions made by other Dream Group members: "We evacuate the bunkers. We bomb the Ho Chi Minh trails, leading from North to South Vietnam. We bomb Hanoi, using a lot of B52's with heavy bombing. I wake up and find John alive and well in the next bunk. The attack was only a dream. I get on the Freedom Bird and fly back to the US."

Dream 20: 04/06/94 Surviving Day Two

Beginning of my first tour. Bus through Saigon to Camp Alpha. The place is lighting up with artillery bursts. I'm one of the last people there. I spend an uneasy night, with the sound of pistol fire (police), the smell of cordite (gun powder); scared shitless my first night there. Wearing my khakis, I get on the bus to the 90th replacement battalion (Long Bin). The squad tents are on the assembly ground in mud. The PX is nearby. My uniform looks neat. I get a Coca-Cola from the PX. I walk over to a group of 10 guys standing near a Coke girl, selling Coke and rice husks. I'm the new guy. They are all ready to go home.

They screw me off because I am the new guy, could get them killed. I get 50 feet away, hear an explosion, get blood, glass, shit all over me. The Coke girl had pulled two grenades. I see an eyeball on the ground. The bodies look gelatinous. Some are still alive, but no one survived. They are all messed up. My uniform is covered with little bits of blood and tissue. I feel dirty, want to get my uniform clean. I pick a guy up. He feels like Jell-O. I think I see him breathing, but he is just shaking.

Suggested changes:

1) Feel lucky instead of guilty.
2) Don't feel guilty; not his fault.
3) Don't have so many people in one place; spread them out more.
4) Have everyone disperse when the spoon on the grenade is pulled.
5) Have the explosion occur in the ice chest. Then it goes straight up, and no one is hurt.
6) Put a long fuse on it; give 15 seconds for them to get away.

The dreamer constructed the following dream, using suggestions from other Dream Team members: "I take a bus ride to Camp Alpha wearing my clean khaki uniform. Three guys are standing around the Coke girl. I am fifty feet away. I hear the spoon on the longer fifteen second fuse. The American soldiers all hear the spoon as well and disperse. The explosion occurs and the Coke girl dies. My uniform is still clean. There are no body parts. I wake up. None of the American soldiers, including the short timers (nearing the end of their tour of duty) are injured."

Dream 25: 05/11/94 Doc's Reward

Fifteen men are at the bottom of a hill with pine trees and bushes, a reinforced squad. The terrain is sandy. We're pinned down by a machine gun operated by two Viet Cong in an open fox hole. A wounded marine is yelling "Doc, Doc!" The fellow next to me catches a round in the forehead that takes his skull off and exposes his brain. His good friend, Mousey (both in the squad for six to eight months), looks at his friend with brain exposed and flips out.

Mousy is low on ammo. He uses half of his ammo in six to seven minutes, is down to his last magazine. He rams the last magazine in his gun and runs straight up the hill toward the machine gun. The gun doesn't hit him; the ends are able to move up. Mousey has run out of ammo by the time he reaches the machine gun. The machine gun is not firing; it is jammed. Mousey leaps across the gun and burns the inside of his legs. He hits the VC with the butt of his weapon, then stabs him with the bayonet. The assistant VC dives into the tunnel next to the VC and disappears. Mousey dives in and kills him too.

Mousey stands on the emplacement while the colonel pins a silver star on. I'm at the bottom of the hill, with the fellow whose skull was taken off. People are yelling "Doc, Doc!," asking me to take care of them. I wake up with feelings of lack of justice, helplessness. Nothing I can do. Feeling the whole weight of the war.

The dreamer proposed the following revised dream after a discussion among Dream Team members: "I get help in the form of helicopters and another corpsman. I get thanks and a citation. Everyone makes it back OK. The squad writes a citation and Mousy awards it to me. The squad members all recover in time to return to the U.S. on the Freedom Bird plane with me."

Dream 27: 05/25/94 Guardian Angel Paul

The helicopters are there. The helicopter is up, but my buddy Paul is still holding onto my hand. They're saying, "He's dead, he's dead." I feel like I'm flying, but I worry about landing on my feet. I go up with him until they say "He's dead"; then I'm floating. The feeling of floating, the sound of the helicopter, and his holding my hand, all stay after I'm awake until I stand up.

Suggested changes:

1) Introducing him to angels, out-of-body experience.
2) He's your guardian angel to protect you.
3) Use the grip as a handshake of encouragement, knowing he's still protecting you.

The dreamer constructed the following revised dream from the above suggestions: "My guardian angel, Paul, is protecting me. He keeps me safe by holding my hand. Holding his hand makes me feel stronger, like a survivor."

Follow-up results for the 6 dreams illustrated above are summarized in Table 2.1, along with the follow-up results from the other 26 dreams in this series. Dream 2, Escape from Pumpkin Hill, did not disappear in the few months of follow-up after the dream revision session, but changed and became less frequent. Dream 7, Thanks from the Past, disappeared as a nightmare. One couldn't be sure within the framework of the Dream Group's duration of operation, with patients coming and going over a period of nine months, that any given dream disappeared totally, but this one was no longer a problem to the dreamer. Dream 13, Mary Ann, also disappeared as a nightmare. Dream 20, Surviving Day Two, promptly changed, with fewer people being killed, and later disappeared. Dream 25, Doc's Reward, initially changed in intensity, allowing the dreamer to fall back to sleep. Eventually, this dream disappeared as a nightmare. Dream 27, Guardian Angel Paul, disappeared as a nightmare.

Essentially all of the illustrated dreams showed some positive change, which was true for the great majority of the 32 dreams in this series. These results are particularly noteworthy when one considers that many of the dreams had been present in a recurrent fashion since the Vietnam War, more than 20 years in the past. These dreams had not faded away on their own, but were firmly entrenched in the minds (brains) of the veterans. The data support the concept that dream revision therapy, also known as imagery rehearsal therapy (IRT), is an effective way of treating recurrent nightmares.[4]

Several principles of successful dream revision for Vietnam veterans with PTSD are well illustrated in the six dreams included in the present chapter. One important principle is putting mangled bodies of fallen comrades back together. This is critical for grieving, which is necessary for successful healing. Dreams 7 (Thanks from the Past) and 13 (Mary Ann) provide vivid examples of the "putting back together" principle.

A second principle is that of bringing in reinforcements, which could take the form of additional soldiers, air strikes, helicopters, rifles, hand grenades, or whatever. Dreams 13 (Mary Ann) and 25 (Doc's Reward) illustrate this. Veterans themselves were especially effective in coming up with ideas, given their familiarity with the details involved in Vietnam combat.

A third principle is to make a slight but crucial change in the combat situation to lessen the trauma. Dream 20 (Surviving Day Two) illustrates this. Once again, veterans were very skillful in this regard, making group therapy potentially quite powerful, as they put their heads together in creative ways. Typically, the dreamer knows that this revision would have made a difference, but doesn't realize he has the power to ask for it. The group enables him to request this change.

A fourth principle is to make a slight but crucial change in the dream symbolism. Dreams 2 (Escape from Pumpkin Hill) and 27 (Guardian Angel Paul) illustrate this. In Dream 2, the addition of foothold steps in the hill enables the dreamer to evade his pursuers. In Dream 27, holding the hand of a dead comrade is transformed from a source of anxiety into a source of comfort.

As it turned out, four participants in the VA dream revision group sessions (providing Dreams 13, 17, 19, 20, 25, 27, 29, and 31 in Table 2.1) were referred to the author for "fee basis" treatment after I left the VA Medical Center, allowing me to follow them over extended periods of time after termination of the dream revision group (see + symbols in the Outcome column of Table 2.1). I had the privilege of working individually in therapy with the dreams of each of these patients, which will be presented in detail in the next four chapters.

TIPS FOR DREAM REVISION FROM CHAPTER 2

1. Dream revision works well as group therapy for veterans from the same war in a VA clinic (or inpatient unit) with multiple facilitators. It

may even be preferable to individual therapy with this population of patients in this setting.

2. The principles of successful dream revision for Vietnam War veterans mentioned above may not all apply to veterans of other wars (Iraq or Afghanistan), for which different principles may need to be developed.

THREE

Postal: Dream Revision for Homicidal Impulses

In the summer of 1994 I finished my residency and fellowship training at UCSD, including work with the VA PTSD programs, and began setting up a private practice in the San Diego community. Over the next few years the VA authorized several of their most challenging PTSD patients to receive intensive treatment from me as a "fee basis" civilian psychiatrist (an outside contractor). The VA did not have the internal resources to provide these patients with the frequency and duration of visits needed to avoid repeated hospitalizations. I was pleased to accept these referrals, as I had come to know the individual veterans well during my three years at UCSD and the San Diego VA Medical Center.

Four veterans from the Dream Team (see Chapter 2) were sent to me by the VA during the period from September 1994 to January 1996. Their stories will be presented in the next four chapters. During the same time period the VA sent me another patient, Tom, not a member of the Dream Team. His story was presented in Chapter 1.

When Carlos first came to my civilian office in September 1994, he was in his early forties. He was Puerto Rican by birth, the youngest of six children, with an extended family still living there. He and his second wife had two young children and would soon be having a third child. Carlos also had three older children from earlier relationships, as well as two grandchildren. One of his older children was a professional soccer player in Germany. Carlos himself had been a welterweight boxer for nine years, with 39 knockouts and 6 decisions (3 for him and 3 against), for an overall record of 42 victories and only 3 defeats. Though not a large man, Carlos worked out regularly, was in good shape, and was wiry, muscular, and a fierce fighter when challenged.

After graduating from high school, Carlos joined the Army in the late 1960s, where he served in the infantry, achieving the rank of staff sergeant. He had several tours of duty in Vietnam, receiving both Silver and Bronze Stars for bravery in combat. Upon his return to Puerto Rico after serving in Vietnam, he was welcomed as a war hero.

Carlos had been psychiatrically hospitalized in San Juan, Puerto Rico in 1972, following a fight with another veteran who pulled a knife. Carlos would have killed the other man if others had not broken up the fight. Carlos was diagnosed with PTSD at that time. He was given the antipsychotic medication chlorpromazine (Thorazine) to calm him down, and had a cardiac arrest, after which he was in a coma for several days. He was psychiatrically hospitalized twice at the San Diego VA Medical Center in 1994.

Prior to his first San Diego hospitalization, Carlos had been working as a mail carrier with the U.S. Postal Service. Veterans were given preference in applications for U.S. government jobs, and many Vietnam veterans (some with PTSD) obtained jobs with the U.S. Postal Service. Carlos's older daughter was scheduled to be married in New Jersey in 1993. Carlos requested permission to adjust his work schedule so he could attend the wedding as the father of the bride. His supervisor denied the request, so Carlos felt that he was being forced to miss the wedding or lose his job. He was furious at his supervisor for this. In January 1994, Carlos became overwhelmed with homicidal feelings toward his supervisor and suicidal feelings toward himself. His friends and relatives, fearful that he was about to "go ballistic" (or "postal") and kill someone, convinced him to present himself voluntarily to the VA emergency room for admission and treatment. Several Vietnam veteran U.S. Postal Service employees had already "gone postal" and killed supervisors and coworkers in the Post Office.

Carlos was admitted to my inpatient PTSD unit early in 1994. He joined our Dream Team as an inpatient. Dream 13, Mary Ann, from Chapter 6 was his dream, presented as an inpatient. Following discharge from the inpatient unit, Carlos stayed on the Dream Team as an outpatient; Dream 31, Escape and Evasion, from Table 2.1 was also Carlos's dream, presented as an outpatient some months later.

Carlos was hospitalized again in August 1994, shortly after I left the VA. By this time Carlos was no longer working with the U.S. Postal Service. This second hospitalization, only six months after his earlier discharge, was due to Carlos's anger at the VA and UCSD for not giving me a faculty appointment at the end of my residency and fellowship. Carlos organized a group of a few hundred veterans who signed a petition to get the UCSD psychiatry department to keep me, but the department had already made hiring commitments to more senior research psychiatrists. PTSD was not a high priority for the department at that time, and my research credentials in psychiatry were modest at best. The VA offered me a position that would have been a step down from what I had been doing, and I chose not to take it.

In September 1994, Carlos became the first VA fee-basis patient in my civilian practice. I wondered whether the VA and UCSD administrators had sent Carlos to me in order to protect themselves from his explosive rage, but I was delighted at the opportunity to work with him. He became one of my most loyal patients, and helped recruit other like-minded anti-establishment Vietnam veterans to my civilian practice. I was not afraid of them because I knew they trusted me to do my best to help them. They had seen dream revision work for other veterans as well as themselves. The VA and UCSD were happy to be free of them, and I was happy to get them. It was a win-win situation for the doctors and administrators, and (perhaps) for Carlos and my other fee-basis patients, though not necessarily for veterans who could not get such fee-basis help.

As additional veterans were referred to me in the period from late 1994 to early 1996, we were able to reconstitute part of the Dream Team in my civilian office. It proved difficult to conduct dream revision group therapy in this less secure setting, as mentioned in Chapter 7, but we were able to have very productive group therapy sessions dealing with current issues, especially relationship issues with spouses, significant others, parents, children, and grandchildren. I continued to work on dreams with my fee-basis veterans, but individually with each veteran rather than in a group setting.

During our session on 3/9/95, Carlos told me many things about his past. He described the large numbers of Vietnamese he had killed and his guilty feelings about this. He told me about his unresolved grief for his mother, who died in Puerto Rico of tuberculosis in 1984. He described his rage at the Post Office, and his gratitude at being hospitalized in January 1994, before anything violent happened. He was doing an excellent job at verbalizing his feelings. Our ongoing discussions about his dreams (see below) may have helped him get in touch with his feelings.

In our session of 4/13/95, Carlos indicated he had recently gotten into a fight with his son's Little League Baseball coach, who had been drinking and said some insulting things about Carlos's son. Carlos punched the man with his left hand and knocked him down. Carlos told me he had shown some restraint; punching the man with his right hand would have been worse. I thought about those 39 knockouts. Later I learned that Carlos's son was taken off the baseball team as a result of the punching episode. His son was angry at Carlos for what had happened. The incident also led to arguments between Carlos and his wife about how to parent their son. Carlos had not had prior experience with adolescent children, his older children having been raised by their respective mothers.

In our session of 4/20/95, Carlos told me how rainy weather brought back memories of the Vietnam War. The brief rainy season in San Diego (typically from December to March) served as a trigger for him. In our session of 4/27/95 Carlos indicated that the bombing of government buildings (by Timothy McVeigh and Terry Nichols) in Oklahoma City on 4/19/95 had given him mixed feelings: sadness for the victims and anger at the perpetrators. He harbored anger of his own toward what he called the "system" (the government), and had thought about blowing up government buildings. He now realized how destructive this could be, and how many innocent victims and their families could be impacted.

In May 1995, Carlos and I were interviewed on a local TV news program that aired at 11 p.m., following a two-hour special program on PTSD in Vietnam veterans. Carlos was interviewed as a veteran suffering from PTSD. He described his symptoms and triggers and his efforts to control his enormous rage. I described the use of group therapy to help veterans like Carlos get rid of their posttraumatic nightmares by changing the endings of the dreams.

Carlos was energized by being on TV. He was excited to realize that his combat experiences, his suffering, and his treatment might encourage other veterans to come forward and get the medical and behavioral treatment they were entitled to. The TV interview was clearly therapeutic for Carlos. Before becoming a PTSD recluse, staying at home in his room much of the time, he had been an outgoing gregarious person, enjoying his notoriety as a military hero and successful boxer. Despite being a PTSD recluse, he had enjoyed being a leader on the Dream Team and had obtained satisfaction from collecting signatures to keep me at the VA. Treatment for Carlos and other Vietnam veterans with combat PTSD was a marathon not a sprint, and we were making headway in his case.

In our session of 6/8/95 I taught Carlos how to use visual imagery to fight off flashbacks of the Vietnam War. He said he would use the image of a park in Vienna where he used to jog. He would work at imaging the details of the park.

In our session of 6/15/95 Carlos reported experiencing grief over his mother's death 11 years earlier and his grandmother's death when he was in Vietnam in the late 1960s. Both had died at about the same time of year, in June/July. Carlos cried in the session and then managed to pull himself back together. In our session of 6/29/95 he expressed his anger at Vietnamese refugees in the United States getting more benefits than Vietnam War veterans. He was letting out his emotions in our sessions rather than keeping them bottled up inside until they caused him to explode.

Our new group, on "interpersonal relations," began in August 1995, about a year after Carlos started therapy with me. Due to several extended trips to Puerto Rico and Tampa, Florida (where his brother lived), Carlos was not able to attend any group sessions until January 1996.

With some interruptions due to his travels to see family, Carlos remained under my care in my civilian outpatient practice for three years, from September 1994 until August 1997, when he and his family moved to Florida, to be closer to his brother and also closer to Puerto Rico, where Carlos planned to have a vacation home. During this three-year period Carlos shared 8 additional dreams with me, giving a total of 10 dreams (2 from the VA hospital Dream Team, Dreams 13 and 31 in Table 2.1, and 8 from my civilian practice). Carlos's 8 dreams from my civilian practice are presented below in chronological order:

Dream 1: 09/14/94 Chased by Skeletons

I am being chased by skeletons in Vietnamese hats and black pajamas, saying "we are the system."

Dream 2: 03/02/95 On the Street

The VA is putting me out on the street.

Dream 3: 03/30/95 Chased by VA

The VA is chasing me, trying to bust me.

Dream 4: 03/30/95 Tied Up

I'm tied up while someone is attacking my kids.

Dream 5: 03/30/95 Child Killed by VC

The VC are killing a child (five to six years old) I knew in Vietnam.

Dream 6: 04/06/95 Drug Dealers

Drug dealers are attacking my mother in Puerto Rico. My brother, my father, and I are defending her. It isn't going well. (I got up to get a drink of milk, then went back into the dream.) I call in reinforcements: Andre and other airborne troops and weapons. We emerge victorious.

Dream 7: 12/05/95 Bosnia

I went to Bosnia as a soldier, said goodbye to my mother.

Dream 8: 07/02/96 Chased by VC (Vietcong)

The VC are chasing my family.

Carlos had a recurrent dream of BEING CHASED (see Chapter 9), either by Vietnamese skeletons or by the "system" (U.S. Army, U.S. Postal Service, VA, UCSD). Dreams 1 (Chased by Skeletons), 3 (Chased by VA), and 8 (Chased by VC) are examples of this recurrent dream in its varying forms. Skeletons and VC (Vietcong) are people he killed. The dreams express his guilt about killing them. The "system" fails to provide the treatment he needs, thereby becoming part of the problem, joining the skeletons and VC as his pursuers. Dream 2 (On the Street) is related to the BEING CHASED dreams insofar as the dreamer, Carlos, is concerned about the VA not providing adequate PTSD treatment, obliging him to come outside the VA to see me.

Dreams 4 (Tied Up) and 5 (Child Killed by VC) seem to be related, in involving children being attacked or killed. These two dreams were shared by Carlos on the same day as Dream 3 (Chased by VA), which connects the three dreams in Carlos's mind. Not only is he BEING CHASED, but the pursuers are after his children as well. Carlos and his wife both expressed concern to me that his rage might put his children at risk, though he had not been physically abusive of them. In Dream 8 (Chased by VC) Carlos's concern is expanded to include his entire family (his wife and children). His PTSD and his anger put all of them at risk.

Dream 6 (Drug Dealers) is the most interesting dream in the series of eight, from the point of view of dream revision. Carlos, his brother, and his father are defending his mother against drug dealers in Puerto Rico. In the middle of the dream Carlos wakes up, drinks some milk, and then goes back into the dream, revising it according to principles he learned on the Dream Team: he calls for reinforcements, including his new friend Andre, whose story is presented in Chapter 4. With the help of his friend, Andre, Carlos is successful in changing his dream. We will see this again in Chapter 4 in relation to Carlos's Dream 31 (Escape and Evasion) from the Dream Team.

On 3/30/95, the day he shared Dreams 3, 4, and 5 with me, Carlos told me about becoming a welterweight boxer. Boxing may have been a symbolic effort to defend himself and his family against pursuers in his dreams. His success in the boxing ring shows his fierce determination to protect his family from the demons of his dreams. Just one week later, on 04/06/95, Carlos finally achieved this in Dream 6, with a little help from his friend.

Dream 7 (Bosnia) reflects Carlos's stress over the ongoing war in Bosnia, which triggered memories of his going to war in Vietnam and saying goodbye to his mother. He indicated that he and his father had been distant when Carlos was growing up. More recently, in the years since his mother's death, Carlos and his father had become friends and enjoyed exercising together and talking about war experiences during their regular visits with each other. His father had PTSD from experiences in World War II (Okinawa) and the Korean War. Carlos's brother in Florida also had PTSD from the Vietnam War.

In our session of 5/31/96 Carlos indicated he had had a hard time with Memorial Day. He remembered his buddies and wondered why he survived and they didn't. He said it helped to come in and see me, and also to help recruit people for our group. He was grateful for the San Diego VA Medical Center, which was better than the one in San Juan. He seemed to be coping pretty well.

In our session of 6/14/96 he told me about a nightmare whose content he couldn't remember, so it isn't included in the list of his dreams. The nightmare was triggered by having a Vietnamese mechanic fix the water pump in his car. Carlos and I worked together on his triggers, which included Vietnamese immigrants, rain, helicopters, loud bangs, sudden movements.

In our session of 11/21/96 Carlos told me about marching in the Veterans Day parade in uniform with all his medals. He felt good about this. It made up in part for the lack of earlier parades. He felt good at the support from the people lining the parade route. He was learning to control his emotions, doing better in the supermarket and at home with family members, though riding the San Diego trolley was still too stressful for him. He was still checking out the "perimeter" of his house at night, looking for possible enemy combatants hiding in the bushes.

In our session of 4/3/97 we talked about Mary Ann, the Vietnam battle that led to his earlier nightmare (Dream 13 in Chapter 2). Carlos was one of only 15 survivors along with 600 dead. We also discussed his near-death experience at the San Juan VA hospital in 1972. Carlos was clearly a survivor. He was beginning to see himself in this way rather than as a victim. The Mary Ann nightmare (Table 2, Dream 13) was gone. He had not had it for several years.

In our session of 6/20/97 Carlos told me about the recent visit of one of his older sons from Germany. Carlos was happy to see his German son, and they got along well together. His son pointed out to the entire family (Carlos's wife and their children) that Carlos seemed to be recovering; he was more mellow, less confrontational. The family members agreed with this assessment.

In our final session of 8/13/97 Carlos and I reviewed his progress over the past three years. He now could see a future and felt hopeful about it. He was looking forward to reconnecting with his childhood, as he would be living in Florida, closer to Puerto Rico, and would be spending more time in Puerto Rico. He was much improved since our first meeting at the San Diego VA hospital back in January 1994.

TIPS FOR DREAM REVISION FROM CHAPTER 3

1. A dream revision strategy used for a combat-related nightmare may prove useful in a civilian-related nightmare as well. Carlos called in reinforcements in Dream 31 (Escape and Evasion) of Table 2 (see Chapter 4 for details). He then used the same technique to protect his mother from drug dealers in Puerto Rico in Dream 6 (Drug Dealers) of Chapter 3.
2. A unique advantage of group therapy for Vietnam combat veterans was the convenient size matchup between the therapy group (6–8 people) and a Vietnam combat patrol. This allowed veterans in the therapy group to establish useful connections between past and present. An example of this is that Carlos, in his revisions of Dream 31 of Table 2 (see Chapter 4) and Dream 6 of Chapter 3, brings in his new friend (Andre) from the current Dream Team as one of his reinforcements.

FOUR

Bubbles: Revising Combat Dreams about Drowning

The U.S. Navy SEALs have recently risen to prominence in our national consciousness following the helicopter raid by a Navy SEAL team in Abbottabad, Pakistan, in May 2011, which resulted in the killing of Osama bin Laden. In my San Diego practice, I had the opportunity to work with Andre, a veteran who had served three tours of duty in Vietnam as a Navy SEAL combatant.

The term SEAL is an acronym for the U.S. Navy's Sea, Air and Land Teams. The SEALs are the Navy's principal special operations force. The SEALs operate at sea, in the air, and on land, but are noted for their ability to work underwater. Andre's dreams, over the 12 years I met with him in my San Diego office, reflected his extensive underwater experiences, some of them traumatic.

The Navy SEALs originated during World War II when the U.S. military recognized the need for soldiers to have assistance in preparing for landings on beaches. In 1943 the U.S. Navy created a series of Underwater Demolition Teams (UDTs) for this purpose. In 1961, President John F. Kennedy, a World War II Navy veteran, spoke to Congress, indicating his deep respect for special forces operations and recommending them for Southeast Asia. The Navy SEAL teams came into being in this context. Initially there were two teams, Team One at the Naval Amphibious Base Coronado, in San Diego, California, and Team Two at the Naval Amphibious Base Little Creek, in Virginia Beach, Virginia. In addition to underwater demolition training, the original Navy SEAL teams received basic indoctrination training at Camp Kerry in the Cuyamaca Mountains in eastern San Diego County.

SEAL training is very rigorous, one of the most rigorous special operations training programs in the world. There are currently at least eight confirmed Navy SEAL teams. The group that killed Osama bin Laden, sometimes referred to as SEAL Team Six (a name now patented by Disney Corporation for marketing purposes), was actually an offshoot of Team Six, known as Naval Special Warfare Developmental Group (DEVGRU), which originated well after the Vietnam War during the U.S. invasion of Panama in 1989.

Andre was in his mid-fifties when I first met him as an inpatient at the San Diego VA Medical Center in March 1994. He had been having both homicidal and suicidal thoughts. His homicidal thoughts had been directed at someone who "punched out" his tires. His suicidal thoughts also involved his car; he was thinking about driving it off a cliff. Andre was African American and muscular, but a bit overweight and out of shape. He was clearly depressed, with difficulty concentrating, difficulty sleeping, loss of interest in activities, reduced energy and motivation. He was also having PTSD symptoms, including nightmares and flashbacks related to Vietnam, withdrawal and avoidant tendencies, and an increased startle response.

Andre served in the Navy for 20 years from the mid-1950s to the mid-1970s (age 17 to 37). Since leaving the Navy he had been doing "bail and recovery" until about 3 years prior to his hospital admission, when a knee operation forced him to stop working. Andre's work in bail and recovery involved apprehending subjects who failed to appear in court, thereby forfeiting their bond. He was what is known as a "bounty hunter," capturing fugitives for a monetary reward from a bail bond company. In 1872 the U.S. Supreme Court gave bail enforcement agents nearly limitless power when hunting down subjects. Andre was a dangerous man, not someone you would want to get into a physical dispute with.

Over the 13 years that I knew and worked with Andre (1994 to 2007) he and I developed a close working relationship. We were almost the same age. As doctor and patient we aged together, sharing insights about the aging process. I helped him through a marriage and subsequent divorce. In our sessions we discussed the quiet pleasures in life, the value of living in the moment. I helped him change back from being a killer and assassin to being a feeling, caring human being.

Andre often had to deal with racism, both in the military and afterward. While in the Navy he developed a close relationship with a white cocombatant in Vietnam, who was killed by a land mine explosion. Andre asked if he could accompany his friend's remains back to North Carolina for burial. The Navy granted Andre's request. He accompanied the bodily remains all the way to the cemetery, but was not allowed to attend the burial because it was an all-white cemetery and Andre was African American. It was helpful to Andre to tell me the story and helpful to me as a white psychiatrist to hear it. Being African American was a challenge for Andre, which he dealt with in the best way he could. This included having white friends as well as black friends.

He told me about another situation when he and two black friends decided to drive from San Diego to New Orleans, two cities where blacks are generally well treated. Unfortunately, as the three men were passing through a rural part of Oklahoma they were stopped by the local police and briefly put in jail as potential troublemakers. Andre was able to secure their release with help from the Veterans' Administration, but this was another unpleasant experience of homegrown American racism for him to share with me.

Andre was born in Jamaica. He lived in Los Angeles until age 9, in Chicago until age 11, and then in Boston through most of high school. He left high school at age 17 in 1954 to join the Navy. While in the Navy, in addition to becoming a SEAL, he finished high school and college, receiving an AA in child psychology and a BS in chemical dependency.

His father died in 1994, shortly after I met Andre at the VA hospital. Andre still had some relatives living in Jamaica. He described being "caned" for infractions at a boarding school in California as a child. He learned to "stuff" his emotions at that time.

It was often hard to know what Andre was thinking; his emotions were not visible on the surface. He could be explosive when his internalized anger became strong enough. This affected his relationships with women. He was married to his first wife for 10 years before they divorced. They had one child, a daughter, now living in Las Vegas near her mother. A son from another relationship died in 1974–75 in a car accident. Andre had twin children from a third relationship: a son living in central California, and a daughter living in Las Vegas. In 2006 he discovered he had another grown son, age 41, with two daughters.

Altogether he had 4 living children, 2 sons and 2 daughters, and 10 grandchildren. Andre was quite involved with his children and grandchildren, often visiting them on weekend trips. For a period of time, 1 of his grandsons moved to San Diego and lived with Andre. Andre's second marriage lasted just a year and a half, from May 2004 to December 2005, during the period when he was my patient. His second wife was Hispanic. She and Andre had dated each other for about six years before getting married.

Andre felt that the marriage ended because of disputes involving his wife's grown children, who did not approve of Andre; he felt their disapproval was racially based.

Andre had diabetes mellitus, for which he took pills. He had knee replacement surgery in 1992 and suffered over the years from intermittent back pain resulting from Vietnam War injuries. He had alcohol abuse problems until his San Diego VA hospitalization in 1994, followed by a four-month admission to the VA alcohol rehabilitation unit in Menlo Park, California in 1994–95. During the years I worked with Andre as an outpatient, from 1995 to 2007, he remained clean and sober.

Andre had a strong tendency to be provocative and confrontational in his relationships with people, both men and women. After becoming an inpatient in our VA PTSD program in 1994 he joined our Dream Team (see Chapter 2). The first encounter between Andre and Carlos (see Chapter 3) was memorable.

By the time Andre joined the Dream Team in March 1994, Carlos had been attending for several weeks and had assumed the position of alpha male in the group. As mentioned, Carlos had been a welterweight boxer and had a definite edginess in his relationships with other veterans. Andre could sense this during his first group session and took it upon himself to needle Carlos, to tease and challenge him. As I later learned, this was Andre's style. He would needle people until they got provoked to fight him. It was not a good idea to get into a fight with Andre. Even Carlos would have had his hands full.

Carlos became quite upset by Andre's needling, and the two came close to blows in our group meeting. We managed to get things calmed down, however, since the two veterans trusted us (myself and the inpatient nurses), even if they didn't trust each other, and the group session continued without further disruption.

Both Andre and Carlos were strong, tough, fearless, decorated combat survivors. It may not come as a surprise to readers that they subsequently became close friends. Both were in my office-based Vietnam veterans group for more than two years, from the time Andre joined the group in 1995 until Carlos moved out of state in 1997.

DREAMS

An interesting instance of the friendship between Carlos and Andre is the following dream **of Carlos's** from the VA dream group, listed in Table 2.1 as Dream 31:

Dream 31: 7/12/94 Escape and Evasion (Carlos's dream, see Chapter 3)

We're getting all our equipment, putting the leach strings on, getting the weapons we needed for the terrain we were going to be in. Going into the canopy. Reconnaissance from Air Force; NVA (North Vietnamese Army) headquarters near there. Destroy them. 6-man team; vicious killers. I was the machine gunner; short-barrel gun is what I used. We started walking. My friend got caught with pungy sticks. We pulled him back. We have to continue the mission. I took the rifle and started walking point. Bamboo release. Disarmed. A few feet more, 500-pound bomb with a trip wire. Bouncing betty. Anti-personnel mine. I found and released 25 booby traps. Got them positioned, and we set up the sniper mission to kill the colonel. Firefight with the NVA. We had to retreat. We killed a lot but had to retreat. Running out of ammunition; fear that someone's behind me. It's still going on. Running; someone behind us. I wake up. Someone coming to get me.

Carlos indicated he had had the dream almost every night for the past six months. Emotions he felt in relation to the dream included fear, anxiety, anger, relief, mistrust, exhaustion, paranoia, and betrayal.

Suggested changes:

1) Another team, including my new friend Andre, comes in to provide support during the retreat.
2) The line company behind us wipes out the NVA.
3) Change the NVA to friendly (U.S.) forces chasing us; they stop when they recognize me.
4) The NVA gives up.
5) Our forces set booby traps; the NVA goes into them.
6) The NVA run into their own bobby traps.
7) There is more light in the dream, signaling dawn.

Carlos selected revision #1, bringing in Andre, his new friend from the Dream Team, to help with the retreat. Following the dream revision session, this dream showed reduced frequency, persisting for some months until finally disappearing.

That Andre could have been helpful to Carlos in fixing his dream is supported by Dream 18 from Table 2, which was Andre's dream:

Dream 18: 3/16/94 Andre's Reality

We're in a Marine forward unit at Three Sisters Mountains. There's a lot of action on the side of the enemy, the North Vietnamese Army (NVA). Our squad is on a search-and-destroy mission. We've been here since dusk, watching and waiting. It's now just before dawn. Three of us are in a bunker with an M60 machine gun. We've strung barbed wire around our position for protection, with empty Coke cans stuck in the wire to warn us of enemies approaching. Suddenly we hear Coke cans rattling. The gunner bolts upright. I check my stoner rifle. The NVA have tripped an air flare. Someone behind us trips another flare. I can see black pajamas (enemy soldiers) like ants. They climb over the wire, forming a human bridge. It's too close to call in artillery. The M60 jams. My stoner barrel gets hot from repeated firing.

I hear cries for "Medics!" Our group charges. It's hand-to-hand combat—my first time. My eyes light on one man in particular. We've shot his legs off with machine-gun fire. He's trying to get his gun, walking on his stumps. I off him with a single shot to the head. I see a look of calm on his face before I shoot him and shatter his face. It looks as if he is saying "Do it!" When I wake up, there's a gunshot. I'm awake.

Andre told us "I'm anxious and disoriented when I get up. I'm sweating and have a headache. I tell myself it's a dream. I've had the dream twice a week since 1975 (19 years). In the dream there's a calm. I wake up before seeing his face shattered. My emotions include anxiety, respect, and guilt."

Suggested changes:

1) Rubberize the Coke cans.
2) A water buffalo rattles the cans.
3) The man with the stumps commits suicide.
4) There are battle sounds rather than quiet calm.
5) The NVA don't make it through wire.
6) The man still has his legs.
7) I can't see the stubby guy's face because it's blanked out by a TV scrambler.
8) We pull back from the perimeter and call in artillery and gunships.
9) Somebody else's gun shoots the stubby man in the head.

10) The stubby man died, getting shot from far away.
11) The stubby man asks me to put him out of his misery.

Andre chose option #7. The most traumatic thing about the dream for him was seeing the man's face shattered. Not seeing the man's face was a great relief. Andre rehearsed the revised dream and indicated that his nightmare of 19 years was gone after two months.

Andre arrived in my civilian San Diego office for the first time in May 1995. He was 58 at the time, single, living alone in an apartment in a southern section of San Diego near the harbor. He was no longer having homicidal or suicidal thoughts but still had flashbacks and nightmares involving combat scenes. He had symptoms of depression, including decreased sleep, decreased concentration, low motivation, and feelings of guilt. His short-term memory was impaired, and he was irritable in his interpersonal relationships with both men and women.

Andre and Carlos were good friends by now and were happy to be the first members of our new outpatient PTSD therapy group. Several other members including Tom from Chapter 1, Gary from Chapter 5, and Jack from Chapter 6, arrived between November 1995 and January 1996.

Andre remained under treatment in my private office (both psychotherapy and medication) over a period of 12 years (Spring 1995 to Spring 2007). We worked together on 19 of his dreams over this extended period. The texts of these dreams is can be seen below. For purposes of analysis I have divided the 19 dreams into four groups, based on events in Andre's daytime life.

Andre's dreams 1–5, from May 1995 to April 1997, occurred during the two-year period from the onset of our outpatient sessions to Andre's sixtieth birthday on 4/9/97. I call this the "**initial**" period of Andre's outpatient fee-basis therapy with me.

Dream 1: 07/18/95 Being Shot At

I'm in Vietnam, being shot at. Can't make it to a doorway.

Dream 2: 08/15/95 People Drowning (I)

People are drowning, flailing near the surface. I'm watching, not doing anything.

Dream 3: 11/03/95 People Drowning (II)

Watching people drown, including kids.

Dream 4: 01/30/96 Snakes in Tunnel

I'm crawling in a tunnel; I can feel snakes under me.

Dream 5: 11/19/96 Climbing the Vietnam Wall

I'm climbing the Vietnam Wall, trying to get up high enough to see a name, but I keep slipping back.

We used each dream as an opportunity for therapeutic intervention. In cases where the dream was clearly a nightmare, we would work at revising it. If the dream was simply interesting or provocative, we might discuss it without trying to change it.

We revised Dream 2 (People Drowning I) by having Andre swimming and helping the people who are drowning. We revised Dream 3 (People Drowning II) by having Andre riding in a patrol boat on the Mekong River and seeing kids swimming and not drowning. We revised Dream 4 (Snakes in Tunnel) by having Andre avoid the tunnel after being warned that snakes were in it. We revised Dream 5 (Climbing the Vietnam Wall) by having a friend at the top of the wall drop a rope so he could pull himself up.

During our session on 4/10/97 Andre mentioned that many Vietnam War era memories were coming back to him. These included a severe fire in 1966 on the USS *Oriskany* (an aircraft carrier), gunboat experiences on the Mekong River, and his visit to the all-white cemetery in Fayetteville, North Carolina (as mentioned above). Andre had just celebrated his sixtieth birthday the day before (4/9/97) and told me "I don't want to live on the edge anymore. I want to live another 30 years. To do this, there are some problems I need to work on." I considered this session to be a major milestone in Andre's treatment. His traumatic memories were coming back, and he was prepared to deal with them. No more avoidance of the past. No more avoidance of the future. He was ready to face his dreams and move forward in treatment. His subsequent dreams seemed more specific, less vague in content. It was easier to identify their origins.

Dreams 6–10 from April 1997 to October 1998, occurred after his reporting of recovered Vietnam War era memories and until the start of his relationship with Gabriella, the Hispanic woman who later became his second wife. I call this the "**pre-Gaby**" period of our therapy together.

Dream 6: 09/23/97 High-Speed Skateboard

I'm on a skateboard sliding at high speed under cars. I'm unable to brake the skateboard and slow down.

Dream 7: 10/23/97 Waterbed Explosion

I'm in an explosion and fall out of my waterbed onto the floor.

Dream 8: 06/23/98 Swimming

Swimming (nightmare).

Dream 9: 07/14/98 *Oriskany* Fire

Fire on the Oriskany *(aircraft carrier, seriously damaged by fire on 10/27/66, with Andre on board).*

Dream 10: 10/06/98 Explosions

I'm hearing explosions in the middle of the night.

Andre said Dream 6 (High-Speed Skateboard) was about trying to buy a car, but finding the prices too high. He decided to back off on that project for a while. In a more general sense, it was about "living on the edge." In our session of 05/06/97 he told me he wanted to get a payee to help manage his money, and I helped him find a dependable person, a nurse at the VA. He had a problem with spending money unwisely, including a gambling problem. Dream 6 reflects Andre's beginning effort to come to terms with money management issues.

Dream 7 (Waterbed Explosion) may have been triggered by a recent MRI Andre had endured; the noises associated with an MRI can sound like military explosions or artillery fire. The dream reminded Andre of the land mine explosion that had killed his white friend, whose remains Andre accompanied to Fayetteville, North Carolina, where Andre was refused entrance to the all-white cemetery.

Dream 8 (Swimming), along with Dreams 2 and 3, was one of Andre's several dreams about swimming (and drowning), to be further discussed below.

Dream 9 (Oriskany Fire) was probably triggered by a recent trip to Florida to help his sister, following a series of summer wildfires that had broken out there. The USS *Oriskany* was an Essex-class aircraft carrier from the World War II era, which operated primarily in the Pacific Ocean into the 1970s, earning battle stars for service in both the Korean and Vietnam Wars. The *Oriskany* fire on 10/27/66, one of the worst shipboard fires since World War II, resulted from the accidental ignition of a magnesium flare. Forty-four men died in the fire. One of these, an officer (ensign), was a close friend of Andre's. Andre was a hero during the *Oriskany* fire, saving a number of lives. He received a citation at the time of the fire, and several other awards later, but felt guilty that he had not managed to save the life of his ensign friend and superior officer.

Dream 10 (Explosions) may have been triggered by hearing a car backfire up close. Andre wasn't sure about any particular Vietnam era precursor for Dream 10.

The importance of the five dreams in the "**pre-Gaby**" group is mostly about recall of Vietnam-era events, as noted by Andre in our session on 4/10/97. The dreams did not offer much opportunity for revision per se, but were important in Andre's overall recovery process.

Dreams 11–16, from October 1998 to March 2005, occurred during the "**Gaby**" period of his developing relationship with and marriage to Gabriella. They met in late 1998 and were married in May 2004.

Dream 11: 06/29/99 Me Drowning (I)

I'm drowning.

Dream 12: 09/06/01 Kid Drowning

I'm in Cambodia, watching this kid drown. I'm face to face with him under the water, almost kissing him. He is wide-eyed. Bubbles are coming out of his nose. I wake up feeling anxious. When will this all be over with?

Dream 13: 09/11/03 Plane Cockpit

I'm in a plane on the ground. We can't get the plane off the ground. I'm behind the cockpit. There is screaming going on. People are trying to gain access to the cockpit. I don't know if the bad guys are in the cockpit or trying to get into the cockpit. There is shooting going past me. I can hear the impact.

Dream 14: 11/18/04 Evil Spirit

There is an evil spirit at the foot of my bed. I can feel its presence. I don't want to put my feet off the side of the bed. The evil spirit starts to press down on my feet. I try to kick it off.

Dream 15: 01/24/05 Water Snake

There is an anaconda in the water. I scream.

Dream 16: 02/24/05 People Drowning (III)

I'm swimming, telling people to stay still in the water so I can finish drowning them.

These dreams are mostly about drowning. Andre revised Dream 11 (Me Drowning I) by making the decision to swim more (at the VA pool) for exercise.

In relation to Dream 12 (Kid Drowning), Andre told me he had been on a patrol in Cambodia: Andre, four other Americans, and a montagnard. He had been standing point. They drowned a Viet Cong family in order to escape detection by the enemy. The woman in the family had a gun. They put the man, woman, and three kids (boys 6 and 8, a girl 14) under water. Andre held the boys. He had been having this dream once or twice a month ever since. We discussed issues of atonement, and methods of dealing with guilt he was carrying from the Vietnam incident. Andre said he was OK with regret but not forgiveness. We did not specifically attempt to change this dream at the time, but agreed to examine the larger issues associated with it in future sessions.

Dream 13 (Plane Cockpit) seems to be an anniversary dream two years after 9/11/01. It was not a recurrent dream for Andre, so we did not try to revise it. Andre had been surprisingly mellow at the time of the 9/11 events: demolition of the World Trade Center towers, extensive damage to the Pentagon, and the loss of 3,000 American lives. As an African American and a Vietnam veteran he had some reservations about justice and fairness in America. As a Navy SEAL, Andre was experienced in setting off explosions. He and other Vietnam veterans had harbored their own fantasies about blowing up various government buildings. In Dream 13 Andre is on one of the 9/11 planes experiencing the stress of the situation. The two-year anniversary of 9/11 seems to be having a stronger impact on him than the original event did. Perhaps this reflects some opening up to current American life as his gradual recovery from PTSD proceeds.

Dream 14 (Evil Spirit) was not recurrent, so we did not attempt to change it but did discuss its possible meaning. He indicated that he liked the night, perhaps because of his background as a Navy SEAL. In the past he had a practice of having an all-night radio talk show on in his bedroom, to ground himself in the present. Sleeping with Gabriella kept him from using the radio in this way, as he didn't want to wake her up. Sometimes he would kick her at night when he was having a nightmare.

Dream 15 (Water Snake) is about an actual incident that occurred on the Mekong River. He had described the incident to me before, but this was the first time he mentioned having a dream about it. Perhaps it would not be recurrent.

Dream 16 (People Drowning 3) seems to be closely related to Dream 12 (Kid Drowning). In our session on 3/24/05, just one month after Dream 16, I suggested to Andre that he try putting all of his swimming/drowning dreams into the present (San Diego, 2005) rather than the past (Vietnam, 1964–1970). He agreed to work on this. Perhaps such a change in venue would help resolve the atonement/forgiveness issue that continued to trouble him.

The last three dreams in the series, Dreams 17–19, occurred after the above suggestion on 3/24/05 and prior to our last session on 4/19/07. I call this Andre's "**mindfulness**" period, as he learned to be in the present moment rather than dwelling on the past.

Dream 17: 04/26/05 Underwater Welding

I'm welding under water.

Dream 18: 07/19/05 Me Drowning (II)

I'm swimming, then drowning.

Dream 19: 09/29/06 Boy Swimming

A boy is swimming, but not drowning. He is breathing and bubbles are rising to the surface.

Dream 17 (Underwater Welding) is interesting in that it combines fire and water, two triggers for Andre (see above). This dream provides a creative blending of the two triggers, thereby helping to bring Andre's nightmares under control: a resolution dream.

Andre provided the solution to Dream 18, plus earlier dreams about himself drowning (Dreams 8 and 11). As a Navy SEAL he had been trained in how to reach the surface of the water when you felt yourself at risk of drowning: let out some air bubbles and follow them up to the surface. He agreed to use this technique in his dreams as well, whenever the issue of possible drowning arose.

In Dream 19 (Boy Swimming) the solution to keep Andre from drowning in Dream 18 can be seen to work for the boy as well. The bubbles rising to the surface tell us that the boy is swimming and not drowning. This is another key resolution dream for the entire series.

Over time, Andre's nightmares diminished and largely went away, though he would occasionally have one when exposed to a trigger, especially fire or a body of water.

To occupy his time, Andre became involved in a series of projects: helping other veterans at the VA, helping his children and grandchildren in various ways, helping girlfriends parent their children, taking care of his plants and his dog, serving as executor of a will, serving as treasurer of the local chapter of a fraternal organization, taking classes in mediation, attending VA-sponsored conferences, reading self-help books, working for a computer repair service.

At our last session, Andre still had a twinkle in his eye. He was coping well with the aging process, serving as the patriarch of his family, involved with a new woman friend, hopeful about the future, yet realistic regarding his emotional scars from military service in the Vietnam era.

TIPS FOR DREAM REVISION FROM CHAPTER 4

1. Look for the simplest change that makes the nightmare go away. This is illustrated in Andre's Dream 18 (Andre's Reality) from Table 2.1, details of which are included in Chapter 4. Using a TV scrambler to blank out the face of an enemy combatant before Andre shoots him (in the face) relieves Andre of enough stress and guilt to make the dream go away. It is important to identify why the nightmare is so stressful to the dreamer. In this case, it was the visual appearance of the combatant's face after being shot.
2. Make use of the dreamer's expertise in devising a dream revision. In the case of Dream 18 (Me Drowning) from Chapter 4, Andre indicated

the technique of avoiding drowning by letting out some bubbles and following them to the surface. The use of this technique helped free him from drowning. As Dream 19 (Boy Swimming) demonstrates, Andre has already learned how to use this technique to save other people from drowning.

FIVE

High Dive: Revising an Interrogation Dream

The U.S. Navy Hospital Corps was established by President William McKinley in 1898 just before the start of the Spanish American War. Navy Corpsmen earned distinction with the Marines on the Western Front in World War I, and hit the beach with the Marines in every battle in the Pacific in World War II. One of the Marines raising the flag at Iwo Jima was a Hospital Corpsman ("medic"). Hospital Corpsmen accompanied Marine units into battle during the Korean and Vietnam wars. Hospital Corpsmen have served in both the Iraq and Afghanistan wars.

San Diego's Naval installations include Camp Pendleton Marine Base, Miramar Marine Corps Air Station, the Marine Corps Recruit Depot, the main Naval Base of the U.S. Pacific Fleet on the west coast, and North Island Naval Air Station. San Diego was clearly a place where a PTSD specialist like myself might be expected to encounter a Marine medic.

Gary was a Marine medic with posttraumatic stress disorder from the Vietnam War. He was the only member of our Dream Team (see Chapter 2) to provide three dreams for deconstruction by the group. Dream 25 (Doc's Reward) from Chapter 2 was Gary's dream. His two other dreams from Table 2.1 (Dream 19 and Dream 29) will be discussed below.

Gary was a very enthusiastic and skilled practitioner of the dream revision method. As a Marine medic he treated combatants in the battlefield in Vietnam. Gary was also a combatant in the U.S. Marine Corps. His battlefield experience and his medical knowledge helped him appreciate the power of dream revision to get rid of posttraumatic nightmares. Hospital Corpsmen are referred to as "Doc" in the field. The job is particularly stressful, since corpsmen are expected to provide medical assistance for severe wounds with only limited medical training.

Following his Dream Team participation in the spring of 1994, plus a few months at the VA's PTSD treatment center in Menlo Park, California, in the summer of 1994, Gary finally obtained approval to join my outpatient practice in November 1995. He was 57 years old, Caucasian, married for the second time, with a total of 12 children, 6 from each of his two wives. Five children ages 13–17 were still living at home. Gary and his family were Mormons.

Gary's dates of military service were from 1956 to 1966 and from 1978 to 1982. His service in Vietnam was from 1965 to 1966. His service-connected medical disabilities included PTSD, tinnitus (ringing) in both ears, decreased hearing in his left ear, and chronic pain from knee and back injuries.

Gary was raised in central California, the oldest of six children. His father was a contractor. A sister died at age 4 (run over by a truck) when Gary was 12. A brother died in Vietnam; a second brother died in a motorcycle accident; and a third brother died in 1997 in Washington State, possibly having been murdered. By 1997, Gary had only one surviving sibling, a younger sister.

Gary was clearly a survivor. During the years between 1995 and 2007 when he was under my care as a fee-basis outpatient, Gary served as a major caregiver for many family members, including his father, his mother, several children, and two grandchildren, one of whom he and his second wife adopted.

Gary's second wife was a nurse. She and Gary seemed to have a strong marriage, though they fought a lot, and he even moved to Hawaii for a few years while she stayed in San Diego. During that time I met with her rather than Gary at his scheduled monthly appointment time. She was quite a few years younger than Gary and initially felt intimidated by him. Over the years she learned to stand up to Gary and even took over the family finances when he became disabled by PTSD. As he recovered under my care, a power struggle developed between them. In couple's therapy sessions I had with them, they worked on "surrendering" to each other, a concept that seemed to work for them. Their marriage did hold together, and they became patriarch and matriarch of a large extended family.

Gary suffered from "anniversary" exacerbations of his PTSD. One anniversary was in September, when he returned home from Vietnam and found his first wife having an affair, which ultimately led to their divorce. In our sessions of 09/19/99, 10/03/02, and 11/07/02, Gary indicated that he understood the basis of his yearly September deterioration. The problem gradually diminished over the years that Gary and I worked together.

Another anniversary phenomenon for Gary was related to the red and green colors of Christmas. He had to retreat to his room to get away from the red/green Christmas decorations. On 12/14/99 he told me that red and green reminded him of blood on olive drab uniforms. Eventually, in our 01/06/05 session, he told me that his family switched from red and green to white and gold for Christmas, which took away his Christmas phobia.

The choice of white and gold was interesting in relation to the family's Mormon faith, since Mormons dress in white robes in their temples and have gold tablets and a gold statue celebrating their angel Moroni. The San Diego Mormon Temple is situated just across Interstate 5 from the VA Medical Center in La Jolla, California, a few miles north from downtown San Diego. I visited the Temple during an open house they held one year while I lived in San Diego. I was able to see the white robes and the gold tablets and statue for myself.

Gary had extensive knowledge about construction techniques. During a four-year period from 2001 to 2005 he had a successful career as part-time high school teacher, making use of his construction skills and disciplined training as a U.S. Marine to work with difficult students in a special school set up for this purpose. He enjoyed teaching construction in this setting; he told me his class had some of the flavor of a boot camp. In our session of 03/06/03 he indicated he had won an award as teacher of the year at his school.

DREAMS

Gary learned the dream revision technique as early as 03/30/94, when we worked on the first of his three dreams with the Dream Team, Dream 19 (Doc Saves a Life), included in Table 2.1. Gary's dream was related to a particular atrocity inflicted upon Vietnamese enemy (Viet Cong or VC) prisoners by U.S. troops. Two VC prisoners would be given a ride in a helicopter. One of them would be questioned about enemy troop positions. If he refused, he would be thrown out of the helicopter to his death. Then the second one would be questioned; usually he would be more cooperative.

Gary recalled this form of torture when in 1966 he himself was kicked out of a helicopter (a "chopper") at 20 feet above the ground by a gunner. Gary said he still harbored a "tremendous sense of anger" toward the gunner. Gary suffered an injury to his left knee when he hit the ground. The pain in his knee subsequently became a trigger to remind him of the helicopter torture.

Dream 19 (from Table 2.1): 3/30/94 Doc Saves a Life

I grab a prisoner and throw him out the door of a helicopter. The prisoner turns into me. I start to float. I can see the tree line, can see the ground and rice paddies rushing toward me. I'm in the crucifix position. Quiet eerie sound.

As commentary, Gary said, "During the dream I have no feelings at first. I see the tree line and get an adrenaline rush, with an overwhelming sense of fear, maybe punishment, helplessness. Where is a safe place to land?"

The Dream Team suggested the following possible changes to the nightmare:

1) Give the prisoner a parachute.
2) Give him a retrorocket.
3) Give him something soft to land in.
4) Have Gary leave the helicopter, so he doesn't see the torture.
5) Have Gary stop the torture.
6) Throw out a dummy instead of a real prisoner.
7) Throw out a soldier of the Army of the Republic of Vietnam (ARVN) instead. [ARVN forces were held in contempt by U.S. forces for being weak, corrupt, and ineffective allies.]
8) Attach a cargo strap to the prisoner, to keep him from falling.

Gary selected revision #5. "Stop the Torture" was Gary's original title for this dream, which he later changed to "Doc Saves a Life." Following the dream group session, this dream was gone within one month.

Dream 25 from Chapter 2, Doc's Reward, was Gary's dream. As mentioned in that chapter, Dream 25 initially changed in intensity after dream revision and then eventually disappeared.

Dream 29 from Chapter 2, Life Prospers, was Gary's third dream from the Dream Team:

Dream 29 (from Table 2.1): 06/08/94 Life Prospers

A fetus rises up out of the dust and gets closer and closer, yelling "Why? why?", louder and louder. There is a sound of snipers shooting in the background.

As commentary, Gary indicated, "We were up at 3:30 a.m. We got to a VC village for a sweep, to burn it down. We came to a straw hut. A woman was in labor, delivering a child. While I dragged her out, the Marine lit the hut on fire. The midwife screamed, 'Don't move her!' I dragged her out into the dirt and tried to help. The rest left and I stayed behind. I had to leave her—the village burning and her having the baby. A lot of the places blew up from stored ammo. I have the dream several times per week. My wife was due to deliver at that time. I have a feeling the fetus is asking 'Why is your life more important than mine? Why did you kill me?'"

In relation to the dream, Gary reported having the following emotions: guilt, survivor guilt, hopelessness, helplessness, and feeling overwhelmed.

Suggested changes:

1) The kid comes back as a young man, and says to Gary, "Why? Why were you so brave to save me?" The fetus changes to the young man.
2) Gary sees the young man at the VA.
3) As Gary wakes up, the voice of the woman says, "Thank you, thank you, thank you."

This dream was gone when I began working individually with Gary 17 months after the Dream Team session. I don't have information as to which changes Gary chose and when the dream actually stopped.

When Gary first came to treatment, he was very irritable and difficult for his family members to deal with. He was autocratic with his children, treating them as if they were military recruits and he were a drill sergeant. He was quite inflexible in dealing with everyday problems. With treatment, he softened, as his wife and children reported. His marriage was often put under considerable strain by his PTSD symptoms. I met a number of times with Gary and his wife and occasionally with one or more of their children. An ongoing source of conflict between Gary and his wife was family finances. Eventually they resolved these issues and managed to keep their marriage together.

Gary had one particular problem which got him in trouble a few times: sometimes he overextended himself. In one particular instance he bought some property in Hawaii and went there to rebuild a cabin on the property. Unfortunately, the rain forest setting in the vicinity of the cabin triggered flashbacks and nightmares from Vietnam, and he had to return to San Diego for emergency treatment. Once back in San Diego, he readily restabilized. After this experience he sold the property in Hawaii and for the most part stayed with his wife in San Diego.

Gary's situation illustrates an important phenomenon about PTSD: namely, that people can sometimes recover remarkably, yet remain vulnerable to a return of symptoms if exposed to triggering conditions reminiscent of their original trauma. An important component in the treatment of PTSD is to help patients identify their triggers. Some triggers can then be avoided completely. Unavoidable triggers can be prepared for, and (hopefully) dealt with appropriately when they occur.

Gary remained under my care as an outpatient over a period of 11 ½ years (fall 1995 to spring 2007). He was very enthusiastic and creative with dream revision, as illustrated by the following dreams which we worked on over the years:

Dream 1: 12/05/95 Lieutenant's Orders

I'm in Vietnam. A PFC (private first class) wakes me up to serve food at 3 a.m., lieutenant's orders. I'm sleeping on K-rations. I refuse. The lieutenant tells me to do it. I check the food and find it unservable. Also, none of the servers is clean enough. The lieutenant has to serve grapefruit slices. I later allow people to eat the food elsewhere.

Gary told me "I was stressed out by recent events in Bosnia, which reminded me of Vietnam." We decided to revise Dream 1 by bringing it from Vietnam into a more contemporary setting: Gary would be working at the Camp Pendleton Marine Base north of San Diego, inspecting the food station there in relation to current deployment of Marines to the newly formed regions of Bosnia, Croatia, and Serbia, within the former territory of Yugoslavia.

Dream 2: 12/09/97 Pond Bombing

In Vietnam, the body of a young boy floats to the surface of a pond after I bomb it.

We changed this dream by having Gary give the boy a weapon to reduce Gary's guilt at killing him. Many Vietnamese women and children carried explosive devices and guns, and posed a significant danger to American soldiers. It was difficult to determine whether a given woman or child was dangerous or not. In such a wartime setting a young boy might have had a weapon.

Dream 3: 04/21/98 Western Gunfight

Willie Nelson and Waylon Jennings with guns, girlfriend with a sick baby. Waylon has a painful illness and asks Willie to kill him. There is a gunfight, and everyone is shot dead except Willie and the baby, who then dies from an illness. Willie is left alone.

Gary told me he was feeling fear, anger, futility, and guilt, concerned about his marital situation, fearful that he and his wife might be breaking up. We decided to change the dream by taking away the guns at the beginning when the singers enter the town, to avoid the shooting. Then Waylon, his girlfriend, and the baby see the doctor, and the baby is cured. Everyone does well (and Gary's marriage survives).

Dream 4: 09/07/99 Immobilized

I'm immobilized. My left little finger is the first thing I can manage to move.

Gary told me that this dream was from Vietnam when a tunnel collapsed on him. In our session of 05/03/01 Gary indicated he was doing fine. His family was doing well. The teaching job was going well; he was adjusting to handling difficult students. He said, "I sometimes dream about Vietnam, but each dream is unique. The repetitive dreams are gone. I have revised all the problem dreams, and they went away. My worst triggers are medic issues." Tears came to his eyes when he said "medic." In order for him to get better, his wife had to relinquish some control. Their marriage was rocky for a time during the transition.

Dream 5: 10/04/01 Son's Helicopter Jump

My son jumps out of a helicopter, rifle in hand. He floats in the air. I'm above the helicopter, watching.

Gary told me that his son was now an Army Airborne Ranger somewhere in or near Afghanistan. It was now just over three weeks after 9/11/01. Gary said, "I feel bad that he had to join the Army to become a man, and now maybe give up his life for it. I was too hard on him when he was younger." We revised the dream by giving his son a rope so he can slide down to the ground safely.

Dream 6: 04/12/02 Killing an ARVN (South Vietnamese Army)

Three of us are standing in a hooch: myself, the lieutenant, and the radio man. An ARVN comes in, armed. He says something to me and the lieutenant about the patrol. I don't trust him, and ask for his ID. I have a weapon too. I am very overbearing. He starts to grab his gun. I threaten him. I go outside. He takes a shot at me. I take a shot at him and kill him.

We discussed the risk of Gary losing his temper during waking life and hurting (or killing) someone. He denied that he was like this in waking life, and his wife agreed with him. This dream didn't need any revision, since Gary has taken decisive action. He is not a victim here, but a survivor.

Dream 7: 01/09/03 Free-fall Dive

I'm falling through the air, in free fall, with my arms stretched out. I'm over water. I go into a forward pike position and make a beautiful dive, with a great big splash.

Dream 7 is a wonderful resolution to Gary's earlier dreams of falling (see above, Doc Saves a Life, Son's Helicopter Jump), converting falling into diving under control.

Dream 8: 02/06/03 Sinking Ship

I'm in a Navy ship, which is sinking. The water is up to the ceiling. I'm breathing the last three inches. The ship continues to go down. I can't escape. I wake up in a cold sweat, unable to breathe.

Dream 9: 02/06/03 Quicksand

I'm in quicksand and can't escape, can't breathe. I'm stuck. I'm being slowly suffocated.

On 02/06/03, when Gary shared Dreams 8 and 9 with me, he indicated that his mother had recently fallen downstairs and hurt herself, fracturing her right arm and right cheek, and having some internal bleeding in her head, which had now stopped. She was 83 years old, now back at home with Gary and his wife, recovering slowly, still confused. Gary felt that Dreams 8 and 9 were about all of their responsibilities (his and his wife's): his teaching, his course work (needed to hold onto his teaching job), his mother, and his granddaughter (living in the home because of her mother's mental incapacity). We concluded that the best way to change Dreams 8 and 9 was to try to reduce his responsibilities, which would not be easy. In this sense, the dreams were providing Gary with useful feedback about his current state of mind.

Dream 10: 04/24/03 Mormon Temple

I'm in the San Diego Mormon Temple. I go to a particular room. I am asked if I will please come to this other room (which doesn't actually exist). They tell me to sit down. All my good friends are there. All the food I like is there. Pretty soon there are 150 people, all people I like. People are talking about things in their lives. What have you been doing? What's going on? There is some talk about the war in Iraq. The meeting goes on for an hour. Such a happy place, so calm and peaceful, so fun to see all my friends. It isn't family or people who died, just friends I like to be around. I feel so safe, so comforted, so loved, to be around all these people.

Gary explained to me that Dream 10 was "incubated" by him in a sense. He told me, "I had tried to dream about a cabin in the woods, with the sound of running water, to calm my anxieties about the war in Iraq, especially the artillery fire filmed by the embedded reporters and shown on TV. This was the dream that resulted, not what I had asked for, but even better. My most powerful experience since Vietnam. Now when I feel anxious, I just remember the dream, and it calms me." Gary's incubated dream had become a source of guided imagery that he could use during waking life to control flashbacks, an important and practical discovery.

During our session of 07/10/03 Gary told me he could now recognize PTSD symptoms when they occur and keep himself under control. He felt good about this, though it had taken 10 years of treatment. During our session of 10/02/03 he told me he felt his PTSD was under control. He could recognize triggers and stand back from automatically responding to them. He was having no nightmares that he could remember. During our session of 01/03/07 he told me that 52 things about Vietnam bothered him. He worked on them one at a time over the years. He didn't have to do them all; the rest fixed themselves.

Dream 11: 03/20/07 Penile Torture

Devised a torture so that someone has the meatus of their penis attached by a nail to a pole, in such a way that they can't stand up without damaging their penis.

Dream 11 may have been related to a trial of the antidepressant, Effexor, which was helpful in reducing Gary's irritability, depression, and pain, but caused some erectile dysfunction. Perhaps Effexor reduced his erection and led to the dream. Gary said that he didn't want to stop Effexor, as it was the best antidepressant he had tried so far. He managed to use dream revision techniques to change the dream, and it went away.

For the most part, I didn't need to help Gary revise his dreams. He had learned the technique on the Dream Team and was quite capable of applying it on his own. Occasionally I would give him suggestions.

In our last session, in April 2007, Gary was still doing well, still taking Effexor. In anticipation of my departure from San Diego, we were transferring care to his new psychiatrist. It was a pleasure for me to see Gary improve so dramatically with dream revision therapy.

TIPS FOR DREAM REVISION FROM CHAPTER 5

1. The method of dream revision can be taught to PTSD sufferers, who then learn to use it on their own. Gary's Dream 7 (Free-fall Dive) is a particularly creative revision of Dream 19 from Table 2.1 (Doc Saves a Life) and Dream 5 (Son's Helicopter Jump), both presented earlier in Chapter 5.
2. Dream 10 (Mormon Temple) was specifically "incubated" by Gary to calm his anxiety. "Incubation" (practicing a positive image) is more commonly used as a technique for combating flashbacks, by having a positive image ready to use in case a flashback should occur at some future time. Dream revision is typically used after a nightmare occurs, to prevent it from recurring.

SIX

Retraumatizaton and Recovery: Vietnam and 9/11

Andre in Chapter 4 had several dreams related to the events of 9/11/01. In the present chapter we will see much more extensive effects of the 9/11/01 World Trade Center bombings on the dreams of Jack, an Army major and highly decorated Vietnam veteran with whom I met weekly to biweekly for 11 years, from 1996 to 2007. We had almost 400 sessions together during this time, the most I have had with any patient in my 25 years of practicing psychiatry. Jack and I began meeting in January 1996. He made considerable progress in therapy over the next 5 years, as his dreams reflect. The events of 9/11/01—and the wars in Afghanistan and Iraq that followed—rekindled his memories of Vietnam, triggering a series of combat nightmares over the next 2 years. Jack provided a total of 41 dreams during our 11-year therapy, which illustrate 1) his initial recovery over 5 ½ years, 2) the return of PTSD symptoms immediately after 9/11, and 3) his subsequent (partial) recovery during a period of 5 ½ years from September 2001 until our final meeting in March 2007.

Jack was 48 years old when he first arrived in my private office in early 1996. I had known him since 1993, when he had been an inpatient at the San Diego VA Medical Center and a participant in the VA dream group (see Chapter 2). Dream 20, Surviving Day Two, presented in Chapter 2, was his dream.

In addition to being a major, Jack was a Green Beret and a recipient of the Distinguished Service Cross (second only to the Medal of Honor), along with Purple Hearts, Silver Stars, and Bronze Stars. As Jack explained to me, he was a "Mustang," having risen in the ranks from enlisted man to officer. Jack weighed 300 pounds when we began our outpatient therapy sessions. He was big and tall, a red-faced, red-haired roly-poly Irishman, with a twinkle in his eye but rage in his heart just beneath the surface. He called himself a serial killer. He did not reveal the details of his killings, but had been involved in search-and-destroy operations (burning down entire villages including women and children), prisoner interrogations, and CIA missions in Europe as a hit man.

I saw Jack frequently because of his volatility. When he could not control his anger, he consented to be hospitalized at the San Diego VA Medical Center. This happened perhaps half a dozen times over the years, usually for just a few days. Although Jack became angry at me personally sometimes, especially when he could sense that my political views were different from his, I never felt physically threatened by him. I could sense the strong affection he felt for me. We both realized that I had probably saved his life more than once.

Jack and his third wife Nancy had been together for nine years before their marriage in 1995. They lived in a rented condominium in San Diego until 1997, when they bought a home in the suburbs. They were devoted to each other but fought a lot. They slept in separate beds for many years due to Jack's sometimes violent nightmares. When getting along, they were sexually active. Jack's primary care doctor prescribed Viagra for him. I prescribed psychotropic medications that did not affect his sex drive. Nancy assisted me on many occasions in keeping Jack out of the hospital. She would sometimes come in with him to our sessions. On other occasions she would call to warn me when Jack was feeling angry or depressed. We managed to avoid any suicide or homicide attempts while Jack was under our mutual care.

In past years, prior to my becoming his psychiatrist, Jack had made several suicide attempts. He told me a story of putting a gun in his mouth and pulling the trigger, but the gun misfired. He threw the gun against a wall and it went off. On another occasion he tried to drive off the Coronado Bridge (which rises high above San Diego harbor, connecting San Diego with the suburb of Coronado) but was stopped by a highway patrolman, a fellow Vietnam veteran. Two additional attempts involved 1) slashing his wrist and 2) trying to pull the wheel and drive a car off the road while a girlfriend was driving.

Jack was tormented by guilt at all the people he had killed and the atrocities he had committed. For the most part, he didn't provide specific details about particular killings or atrocities. We dealt with such material through his dreams, which were colorful and often metaphorical. Jack liked to talk metaphorically as well. It served his need to maintain a semblance of confidentiality. In this sense Jack seemed an ideal candidate for dream revision therapy. Jack's goal in our outpatient sessions was to be transformed from a killer, a "wolf-man," with an angry impulse to tear out someone's throat, into a "silver fox," a highly decorated officer and elder statesman who had put his tumultuous past behind him.

Jack's early childhood years were spent in Los Angeles. He was the oldest of five children, with two sisters and two brothers. Jack's father had been in the military as well and had been both an alcoholic and a womanizer. Jack's parents were caught up in the LA social scene and turned Jack over to his maternal grandparents for extended periods of time. Jack resented this, but benefitted emotionally from the contact with his grandparents. His maternal grandfather became a major role model in his life. As a child, Jack contracted polio and spinal meningitis and spent a year at LA General Hospital.[1] Jack's grandparents came every week to see him, but his parents only came four times. Jack remained angry at his parents over this neglect.

The family moved to Las Vegas for Jack's teenage years. He was state boxing champion in Nevada from age 14 to 17. He was a golden glove welterweight boxer in high school at 147 pounds, in addition to playing on the football team and performing in the musical "South Pacific." He started college, but dropped out after his girlfriend broke up with him. He joined the Army at age 18 and had two tours of duty in Vietnam, 1966–67 and 1968–69. He was an Airborne Ranger in the Army, involved in mine clearing, indigenous liaison, criminal investigation, and cryptography. He was medically evacuated out of Vietnam in 1969, blinded and wounded in the legs. Metal fragments were removed from his eyes. He received this treatment in San Francisco; the first thing he saw when recovering was the Golden Gate Bridge. After the war, serving in the military police in Washington, D.C., he was involved in riot control. He also spent some time in Europe, working with the CIA. He told me once about getting shot in the stomach in Istanbul.

He remained in the Army for 10 years, from 1966 to 1976. By the time Jack left the Army, he was already having symptoms of posttraumatic stress disorder (PTSD) and drinking too much. He went AWOL for more than a month at the end of his military service in 1976. He was hospitalized in Ohio in 1977 for bizarre behavior and at the Long Beach VA in California in 1982 for alcohol rehab. The Long Beach VA admission was after the failed suicide attempt with the gun in his mouth. He remained sober after the 1982 hospitalization, attending Alcoholics Anonymous (AA) regularly and serving as a sponsor for many people. He was hospitalized at the San Diego VA six times between 1993 and 1995 for homicidal and suicidal ideation. He spent five months in 1994 at the VA's PTSD rehabilitation hospital in Menlo Park, California.

Jack had been married three times. Unlike his father, he remained faithful to all three wives. He had two children, a boy and a girl, from his first marriage. His first wife left him because of his drinking. Jack indicated that over the years he had fathered three or four illegitimate children whose whereabouts he did not know.

He had a heart attack in 1986 from which he fully recovered. He had a cancer of the colon resected in 1990, from which he likewise recovered; a colonoscopy in 1998 was negative. Jack struggled with obesity during the years I worked with him, regularly attending Overeaters Anonymous (OA) beginning in 2000. His weight increased to 443 pounds before he started OA; he was able to bring it down to 230 by September 2005, at the time of his five-year anniversary with OA.

As he began to recover in treatment and lose weight, he would come in nicely dressed, wearing a black leather jacket, or perhaps a maroon V-neck wool sweater, along with dark pants and dress shoes. He indicated he was on his way to an OA meeting after his session with me. Getting dressed up reminded him of his past lifestyle in Las Vegas, drinking, partying, dating several women at the same time.

After five years in therapy with me, from 1996 to 2001, Jack seemed to be recovering well. Then, on 09/11/01, the World Trade Center towers in New York City and the Pentagon in Washington, D.C., were bombed by terrorists flying commercial U.S. airplanes. Jack was enormously impacted by this event. He was similarly impacted by the resulting wars in Afghanistan and Iraq.

JACK'S DREAMS

During the course of his 11-year therapy, Jack shared 41 dreams with me. The dreams are listed in Table 6.1.

Dreams 1–15 (from 04/97 to 04/01, 4 years) constitute **Group 1 (Pre-9/11)**, beginning after Jack's father's death in March 1997 and ending a few months before the World Trade Center bombings in September 2001. Dreams 16–22 (from 10/01 to 03/02, 5 months) constitute **Group 2 (Afghanistan War)**, beginning after the World Trade Center bombings and ending a few months before the election of Hamid Karzai by the Loya Jirga (grand council) as head of state in Afghanistan in June 2002. Dreams 23–32 (from 09/02 to 12/03, 15 months) constitute **Group 3 (Iraq War)**,

Table 6.1 Dreams in a Mustang Major with PTSD

#	Date	Dream Title	Lines	Theme
1	04/25/97	kill my mother I	1	combat/mother
2	02/02/99	shark attack*	4	Vietnam
3	09/21/99	fire from the sky	1	Vietnam
4	10/05/99	skinned alive*	1	Vietnam
5	12/10/99	boy soldier*	2	Vietnam
6	02/15/00	honor guard#	3	military
7	02/22/00	tornado	3	parents
8	04/18/00	killed	1	combat
9	10/31/00	rescuing my family	1	family
10	11/28/00	helicopter help#	1	Vietnam
11	01/09/01	eating, drinking, smoking	1	eating
12	01/16/01	wife's infidelity	1	wife
13	02/20/01	wife is leaving	1	wife
14		waiting in ambush	1	Vietnam
15	04/03/01	dead people return	2	Vietnam/family
16	10/02/01	Afghanistan I#	11	Afghan/Vietnam
17	10/09/01	Afghanistan II#	18	Afgh/Viet/father
18	10/16/01	in paradise	5	wife
19	11/27/01	firefight I#	11	Vietnam/father
20	03/12/02	Puerto Vallarta	3	wife
21		Ireland	1	wife
22		Belize	2	wife
23	09/13/02	Nazi youth camp#	7	World War II
24	01/03/03	shackled in Vietnam	9	Vietnam
25	01/24/03	desert battle I	3	Iraq
26	01/31/03	desert battle II	3	Iraq
27	03/28/03	Iraq war officer	5	Iraq
28	04/25/03	Vietnam/desert	4	Iraq/Vietnam
29	08/29/03	family baseball	3	family/wife
30	09/19/03	Vegas good life	3	sex
31	11/14/03	firefight II	4	Vietnam

(Continued)

Table 6.1 (Continued)

#	Date	Dream Title	Lines	Theme
32	12/05/03	firefight III*	4	Vietnam
33	01/09/04	sexual dreams I	1	wife
34	04/23/04	just say no#	4	military
35	07/30/04	seeking Bin Laden#	6	Afghanistan
36		sexual dreams II	2	sex
37	02/04/05	drinking and whoring	2	father/sex
38	07/22/05	D.C. military#	4	military
39	12/09/05	wife left and returned	2	wife
40	03/30/06	in combat	1	combat
41	11/17/06	kill my mother II	2	combat/mother

Asterisks (*) in Table 6.1 refer to dream revision training sessions. Number signs (#) in Table 6.1 indicate successful dream revisions. For ease of presentation, the 41 dreams in Table 6.1 have been divided into four groups.

beginning after Hamid Karzai's election and ending just before the capture of Saddam Hussein in Iraq in December 2003. Dreams 33–41 (from 01/04 to 11/06, 2 years and 10 months) constitute **Group 4 (Post-Capture of Saddam Hussein)**, beginning 4 months after the capture of Saddam Hussein and ending 4 months before our last therapy session in March 2007.

We will focus our attention on the war-related dreams in each group, which constitute 24 out of the total of 41 dreams. (Two war-related dreams were left out as being too brief and too vague to analyze.) Table 6.2 lists Jack's 24 war-related dreams in chronological order, subdivided into the four groups described above. Dreams in each group will be presented and discussed together.

Group 1 (Pre-9/11)

Dream 1: 04/25/97 Kill My Mother (I)

I kill my mother. My father says "this one is mine; the rest are yours."

Dream 2: 02/02/99 Shark Attack

I'm swimming off the coast of Vietnam, out to the two-mile buoy, heading for the hospital ship, a mile further out. I'm attacked by a shark/whale,

Table 6.2 War-Related Dreams (n=24)

#	Date	Dream Title/Period	Group	Months
	[4/97 to 4/01	**Pre-9/11]**		**48**
1	04/25/97	kill my mother I	1	
2	02/02/99	shark attack*	1	
3	09/21/99	fire from the sky	1	
4	10/05/99	skinned alive*	1	
5	12/10/99	boy soldier*	1	
6	02/15/00	honor guard#	1	
10	11/28/00	helicopter help#	1	
14	02/20/01	waiting in ambush	1	
15	04/03/01	dead people return	1	
	[10/01 to 11/01	**Afghanistan War]**		**1**
16	10/02/01	Afghanistan I#	2	
17	10/09/01	Afghanistan II#	2	
19	11/27/01	firefight I#	2	
	[9/02 to 12/03	**Iraq War]**		**15**
23	09/13/02	Nazi youth camp#	3	
24	01/03/03	shackled in Vietnam	3	
25	01/24/03	desert battle I	3	
26	01/31/03	desert battle II	3	
27	03/28/03	Iraq war officer	3	
28	04/25/03	Vietnam/desert	3	
31	11/14/03	firefight II	3	
32	12/05/03	firefight III*	3	
	[4/04 to 11/06	**Post-Capture of Saddam Hussein]**		**34**
34	04/23/04	just say no#	4	
35	07/30/04	seeking Bin Laden#	4	
38	07/22/05	D.C. military#	4	
41	11/17/06	kill my mother II	4	

*dream revision session
#successful dream revision

torn apart and swallowed, but somehow I survive, in great pain. I don't want to live like this.

Dream 3: 09/21/99 Fire from the Sky

It's Vietnam. Fire comes down from the sky. Everyone dies except me.

Dream 4: 10/05/99 Skinned Alive

I'm in Vietnam, getting skinned alive and dismembered.

Dream 5: 12/10/99 Boy Soldier

I'm in Vietnam. I see a soldier with hand grenades. I shoot him. It turns out to be a nine-year-old boy.

Dream 6: 02/15/00 Honor Guard

I'm in the honor guard at the White House (during the Johnson or Nixon presidency). I'm dressed all in white, with gold trim, but I can't find my pants. I'm frantic about it. Then I wake up.

Dream 10: 11/28/00 Helicopter Help

My squad comes in by helicopter.

Dream 14: 02/20/01 Waiting in Ambush

I'm hiding in a rice paddy waiting to ambush VC.

Dream 15: 04/03/01 Dead People Return

Several people who have died (my father, maternal grandfather, a Vietnam War buddy) come back to life, and seem to be doing fine.

Jack shared Dream 1 (Kill My Mother I) with me shortly after his father's death in March 1997. Jack told me he had not been invited by his family to attend the memorial service. At the time he shared Dream 1 with me (4/25/97) he indicated he was still angry with his mother. Interestingly, he had almost the same dream about killing his mother more than nine years later, at the end of the dream series (see Dream 41, Kill My Mother II). Important differences between the two dreams are that Dream 1 is (probably) set in Vietnam and involves Jack's father, while Dream 41 is likely set in Iraq and does not involve Jack's father. The idea of killing his mother has not changed in Dream 41, but Jack has now taken the job away from his father.

Jack said he had had Dream 2 (Shark Attack) three or four nights per week for many years. We revised it by replacing the shark with a rubber boat that picks him up and takes him out to the hospital ship for an ice cream party (his idea). He has a good time with the crew. Then they take him back to the beach.

Dream 3 is reminiscent of Jack's dream in Chapter 2 (Dream 20, Surviving Day Two) in that there is an explosion, and everyone dies except him. Later on in the present series (Dream 16), Jack seems to have a revised version of that earlier dream from the Dream Team.

Dream 4 (Skinned Alive) was revised by having Jack's squad of five men get rescued by a helicopter. Dream 5 (Boy Soldier) was revised by making it clear that the boy is dangerous and needs to be killed. Both of these revisions seemed to work, at least for a while, until triggers brought them back briefly.

Jack said that Dream 6 (Honor Guard) seemed to be "about the purity of my motives (white) plus the honor of my accomplishments (gold)." He felt good about the dream, but indicated "I still need to get my pants back. First I need to lose more weight."

Seven months after telling me Dream 6, in September 2000, Jack started going to Overeaters Anonymous (OA) in an effort to lose weight. We developed the metaphor that he was shedding guilt about Vietnam as he was shedding pounds in OA. This metaphor seemed to be helpful to him.

In addition, OA got him to start thinking about love rather than mayhem and violence. I encouraged Jack to be loving and caring rather than angry and hateful. Our therapy became a kind of reverse bootcamp, changing him back from a killing machine into a human being. It is interesting to wonder whether cutting down on red meat as part of his OA diet might have contributed to this.

Dream 10 (Helicopter Help) is possibly the revised dream that Jack and I called for after Dream 4 (Skinned Alive). One can't be sure about this, but Dream 10 does not seem to be a nightmare, in any case.

Dream 14 (Waiting in Ambush) is positive in that Jack is on the offensive rather than the defensive. Dream 15 (Dead People Return) has positive features as well. Jack's father returns from the dead along with other major male figures in Jack's life (maternal grandfather, Vietnam War buddy).

The last three dreams in the series (10, 14, 15) are certainly more positive than the first four dreams (1, 2, 3, 4), with Dreams 5 and 6 as transitional. One could make a case that Jack's dreams indicate some recovery from PTSD, which in fact was the case in Jack's waking life.

Group 2 (Afghanistan War)

Dream 16: 10/02/01 Fighting in Afghanistan I

I'm an operative in the Special Forces in Afghanistan, trying to get bin Laden. I am with these old guys that I knew, wearing our jungle outfits from Vietnam. It's hot as a son-of-a-bitch. We are attacking a village. Here we fucking go again, getting into a war we can't win. There are six of us. Almost immediately two men get killed. There are four of us left. I step on a mine. It goes click. If I release the pressure by removing my foot, it will explode. One of my buddies comes over, puts a knife under my shoe and resets the mine. I move away. Then he puts some C4 explosive on the mine to blow it up. It makes a big hole in the sand when it blows up.

Dream 17: 10/09/01 Fighting in Afghanistan II

I'm with a group going into Afghanistan. All guys I know. They are all dead, killed in Vietnam. I'm with my father too. We're attacking, setting explosives, blowing up the place so we can get big equipment in. Firing, killing the sons of bitches. Using M16s, M60s, mortars, modernized since Vietnam. The Russians are on our side this time, as well as the English, French, Germans, Australians, Koreans. I see the old red stars painted out, replaced by the blue UN symbol. Attacking, pulling up on their flanks, running them back into the woods. A hilly area with white rocks. They run. I'm the leader. It's gut-wrenching. I'm afraid if I make a mistake, someone is going to die. The first object of the mission is to get home alive.

I come out all messed up, thoroughly wounded, with an eight-month recuperation time (just like before). My father is my counselor, my conscience. I'm sitting in a wheelchair, looking over a bunch of sand, a bay with water in it. I feel a dog lick my leg.

Dream 19: 11/27/01 Firefight I

I'm in the midst of a firefight, blocked in on both sides, 10 of us, 400 of them. It's a fair fight because of our technology (Claymore mines are already out there). The enemy are not good shooters. People are being blown up. I have blood all over my hands and face. I'm sticky with blood. I'm the head of the squad. There isn't enough time for me to do all this. I delegate to the others, who are all experienced. We are an elite team. I look over and see my father there, saying "Go get 'em." He isn't in uniform. I say, "Get the hell out of here; you don't belong here." When I start talking to my father, I wake up.

Following the bombings of the World Trade Center and the Pentagon on 09/11/01, the armed forces of the United States, Great Britain, and the Afghan United Front (National Alliance) began an invasion of Afghanistan on 10/07/01 known as Operation Enduring Freedom. The bombings in New York City and Washington, D.C., were thought to be the work of Osama bin Laden and his Al Qaeda organization, whose headquarters were thought to be in Afghanistan near the border with Pakistan.

Dreams 16 (Fighting in Afghanistan I), 17 (Fighting in Afghanistan II), and 19 (Firefight I) clearly relate to these events. Unlike Luis in Chapter 7 (see below, Dreams 1 and 2), who had nightmares about the actual World Trade Center bombings, Jack's response to 9/11 is to dream about combat, transferring his Vietnam combat experiences to Afghanistan. Jack's father who had died 4 ½ years earlier, has returned from the dead (see Dream 15) and is fighting along with him, serving as his conscience (Dream 17), encouraging him to fight (Dream 19). After Vietnam, Jack was ostracized by his father and his father's friends because of atrocities he had committed. They had accused him of going "Asian." 9/11 seems to free Jack from some of his Vietnam War guilt. Killing is now acceptable again.

Though these dreams are about combat, they are not really nightmares for Jack. He is neither a helpless victim nor a guilty perpetrator. He is just taking care of business (like Bret in killing the Junkyard Dog in Chapter 9). In Dream 16 he even manages to avoid injury by having his buddy use a combat trick to defuse a land mine. Dream 16 seems like a revised dream when we compare it with the revised version of Jack's dream in Chapter 2 (Dream 20, Surviving Day Two). In the revised version of Jack's earlier dream the explosive device is given a longer fuse to allow Jack's American buddies to get out of range before it goes off.

Dream 17 feels like a revised dream as well, in that his father is his counselor rather than his critic. Jack does not go "Asian" in this dream. Dream 19 also feels like a revised dream in that Jack's father is supportive, saying "Go get 'em."

Group 3 (Iraq War)

Dream 23: 09/13/02 Nazi Youth Camp

I'm in a Nazi concentration camp for youths, to build them into soldiers. They are transplanting brains, cloning people, building robots, a conveyer belt system. They are wearing military khaki uniforms, with white ascots and berets. The youths are getting educated, receiving degrees. The Nazis are intent on becoming world conquerors. I wake up, feeling this is weird and frightening.

Dream 24: 01/03/03 Shackled in Vietnam

I'm shackled, both hands and feet. We're in Vietnam. I have a rifle, a steel pot (helmet with camouflage). Mortars are going off. It's nighttime. VC are coming through the wire, throwing saps and grenades. I'm trying to get to the berm, going down a hill to get to the perimeter. Rockets are shooting through hooches, blowing them up. One blows up the mess hall and kills the cook. I finally get to the berm. People are yelling at me, "Where were you?" I am beside myself. I feel ashamed.

Dream 25: 01/24/03 Desert Battle I

I'm being gassed while attacking in the desert. I have a gas mask on. I develop boils on my neck, scratchy throat, bloody nose. I'm trying to get everyone to leave the area. We retreat and I die.

Dream 26: 01/31/03 Desert Battle II

I'm fighting a war in the desert. Diesel smell of the tanks. Dry mouth, cracked lips, heat. I wake up and say I don't belong here. I laugh; this is funny (though it was frightening at the time).

Dream 27: 03/28/03 Iraq War Officer

I'm in my thirties, though the setting is now. I'm joining the Army for the Iraq War. I have to take a battery of officer candidate tests. If I score 15 or above, I'm in. I score 24, and they say that I'm going to officer candidate school. I wake up, saying, "Oh shit!" I don't want to do it.

Dream 28: 04/25/03 Vietnam/Desert

I'm back in Vietnam. It's mixed up with the desert. Suicide bombers are coming at me. I shoot them in the head. Their blood spatters all over me. I'm cutting off heads, doing atrocities, just like in Vietnam. I'm full of madness.

Dream 31: 11/14/03 Firefight II

Floating heads, cutoff heads, limbs, a child running, with his arm spurting blood. Someone kills him—it could be me. We're in the middle of a firefight. Blood, guts, smoke, fire. Helicopters coming down, firing at them. I feel trapped. Then I wake up.

Dream 32: 12/05/03 Firefight III

We're in the midst of a firefight. I see a naked little Vietnamese girl running, blood spurting out from her shoulder, where her left arm had been ripped off. I shoot her to put her out of her misery. I wake up in a cold sweat.

Dream 23 (Nazi Youth Camp), reported on 09/13/02, may be a 9/11 anniversary dream. Jack's comment regarding this dream was as follows: "A part of me wants to control the whole world to my liking, but I reject the Nazi methods. I believe in freedom and independence, which is the American way." Dream 23 is a key dream in Jack's recovery. It is related, I believe, to his involvement in Overeaters Anonymous (OA), which has been very humanizing. He has learned to love people in OA, empathizing with their suffering and their efforts to lose weight. He rejects the process depicted in the dream. In real life he is serving as an OA sponsor and lecturer, a 12-step enthusiast. In OA each person is respected as an individual, with his/her own cravings and addictions.

The key to Dream 24 (Shackled in Vietnam) is the shackles. We can only speculate as to what they might represent. Perhaps just the partial paralysis that is known to occur in REM sleep;[2] many people without PTSD have dreams of being paralyzed. Jack had on occasion acted out his dreams and even injured his wife Nancy in the process. Perhaps his recovering brain is putting some restraints on his behavior.[3] Obesity is a possible source of his shackles. His weight was 280 at the time of this dream, well above his combat weight of about 180, but below his reported maximum weight of 443 several years earlier. The shackles could be Jack's psychotropic medications (lamotrigine, nefazodone, thioridazine, clonazepam) acting as "chemical" restraints on his behavior. It is difficult to say for certain.

Dreams 25 (Desert Battle I), 26 (Desert Battle II), 27 (Iraq War Officer), and 28 (Vietnam/Desert) all take place in the desert, suggesting the war in Iraq. The actual invasion of Iraq by U.S. and UK ground troops began on 03/20/03, after Dreams 25 and 26 but before Dreams 27 and 28. The invasion was anticipated and widely discussed in the news media some months before it actually occurred, and Jack's dreams reflect his anticipation. The major combat operations of the war were completed by 05/01/03, after Dreams 27 and 28.

The Iraq War is less stressful to him than the Vietnam War was, since he watches it from his living room. He could be one of the military advisers they had on TV: generals, colonels, majors. He explains to me about paratroopers. He was in the Green Berets, Airborne Rangers, Special Forces. The encouraging thing about Dreams 25, 26, 27, and 28 is that they are all set in the present (the desert in Iraq) rather than the past (the jungle in Vietnam).[4]

Dreams 31 (Firefight II) and 32 (Firefight III) are about Vietnam, but may have been triggered by the Cedar Fire in San Diego County, first discovered and reported on 10/25/03, fully contained on 11/03/03, and brought under complete control on 12/05/03. The Cedar Fire, which burned over 280,000 acres, including 2,200 homes, and killed 15 people, including 1 firefighter, was at the time the largest fire in recorded California history. Jack's house was not damaged by the fire, but some houses in his neighborhood were burned to the ground. Jack said to me, "I drove down Highway 52 after the fire. It looked like it had been napalmed. I also watched war movies on Veterans Day."

Dream 32 (Firefight III) was a recurrent nightmare for Jack. He felt guilty for putting another human being out of her misery: "I did an inhuman thing, treating her like an animal: a dog or a horse." This dream may have served as a "screen" for atrocities Jack committed during the war.[5] Compared to them, his action in this dream is less objectionable.

We discussed possible revisions to Dream 32. What about making the girl American (and male)? Jack admitted killing several American soldiers who asked to be killed due to the severity of their wounds. He did not feel guilty about killing them. If he had not killed the girl, she would most likely have died anyway, or one of his men would have killed her. If he had tried to save her, he could have gotten killed himself, since they were in a firefight. In the end, we decided not to change the dream. Just discussing it had helped Jack let go of it. He did not report having it again.

Group 4 (Post-Capture of Saddam Hussain)

Dream 34: 04/23/04 Just Say No

A coalition of people want me to do a hit. It's like the mob or the CIA. I'm having difficulty with my conscience. I don't want to do this. I don't want to kill anybody. People are disappointed in me. I maintain my position. I stand up to them.

Dream 35: 07/30/04 Seeking bin Laden

I'm in the Middle East in the CIA, disguised as an Arab, looking for bin Laden. My skin has been darkened. My hair has been blackened. I look the part. We're trying to find someone we can bribe. Terrorists are all around us, carrying weapons: automatic weapons, bombs, mines, grenades. My heart is pounding. Fuck! What am I doing here? I wake up out of bed.

Dream 38: 07/22/05 D.C. Military

I'm working in D.C.: at the Pentagon, the White House, the Capitol building, embassies. Different generals are trying to get me to go with them, to be their aide. Each one says that I would be able to advance with him.

Dream 41: 11/17/06 Kill My Mother

I'm in combat, going through houses. I end up killing my mother. I feel bad about this.

Group 4 dreams, after the capture of Saddam Hussein on 12/13/03, tend to be less combat-ridden than **Group 2** or **Group 3** dreams. Jack seems to be back in the recovery mode that we saw in his **Group 1** dreams. Dreams 34 (Just Say No), 35 (Seeking bin Laden), and 38 (D.C. Military) seem to reflect our dream revision therapy efforts. In Dream 34 Jack indicates his killing days are over: "I don't want to kill anybody." In Dream 35 he says essentially the same thing: "What am I doing here?" In Dream 38 he seems to be resisting the efforts of generals to recruit his services. The dream does not make clear what those services might be: returning to his CIA activities, as in Dream 35? Jack does not seem to be tempted.

In Dream 41 (Kill My Mother II) Jack feels bad about killing his mother. In Dream 1 (Kill My Mother I) he did not report feeling bad about killing his mother. Jack had ambivalent feelings toward his mother. In our session of 01/29/98 he said he had called his mother and told her he loved her. On

12/08/98 he told me he had been ripped off by his mother, sisters, and brother for more than $65,000. On 08/27/04, just a few months before the presidential election, with George W. Bush (the Republican, a National Guardsman during the Vietnam War) against John Kerry (the Democrat, who served in Vietnam), Jack indicated angrily that his mother was a Democrat. We laughed together when I (a Democrat) admitted that my mother was a Republican. This was clearly the American way.

GENERAL COMMENTS

After 11 years and 400 sessions, Jack's therapy was not yet completed in 2007 when I left San Diego. He made important progress in the first five years of treatment from 1996 to 2001. This progress is evident in his dreams of **Group I**.

The terrorist bombings of 09/11/01 in New York City and Washington D.C., and the wars that followed in Afghanistan and Iraq, triggered a series of combat nightmares that are included in Jack's **Group 2 and 3** dreams during the two-year period from late 2001 to late 2003. These nightmares were stressful to Jack, but allowed him to utilize dream revision skills he had learned during our first five years of therapy. The **Group 2 and 3** dreams marked by number signs (#) in Tables 6.1 and 6.2 show indications of having been the products of dream revision therapy (see above comments regarding Dreams 16, 17, 19, 23, and 32). Jack emerged from this two-year period more determined than ever to pursue his goal of becoming a "silver fox."

The capture of Saddam Hussein on 12/13/03 was a reassuring event for Jack. I wonder how he would have felt about the killing of Osama bin Laden on 05/02/11. Jack was interested in the capture or killing of Osama bin Laden, as his Dreams 16 (Fighting in Afghanistan I) and 35 (Seeking bin Laden) suggest. However Jack's **Group 4** dreams, especially Dreams 34 (Just Say No), 35 (Seeking bin Laden), and 38 (D.C. Military), document his acceptance that his active duty military days were over, and had been over for many years (since 1976).

General Douglas MacArthur famously said of himself that "Old soldiers never die; they just fade away." Jack's PTSD seemed like this to me by the time our sessions stopped in 2007; it was gradually fading away. This reflects the value of our treatment sessions, since PTSD once established does not usually just fade away; if left untreated, it gets worse and worse.[6]

Jack's PTSD was mostly fuelled by guilt. Dream revision alone cannot eliminate guilt of the magnitude that Jack was dealing with. He needed to supplement dream revision by taking action in waking life, namely, by showing love and kindness toward other people, letting go of the wolf-man inside of him. His involvement in OA helped with this. Jack also became involved in Catholic Church activities in an effort to deal with his "sins" and his guilt about them. He had made significant progress in 11 years, and fortunately was still alive to continue in his recovery program.

TIPS FOR DREAM REVISION FROM CHAPTER 6

1. Jack's dreams, 41 in all, cluster into four temporal segments (**Groups 1–4**) in relation to three key events in the public arena: the World Trade Center Bombings in September 2001 (separating **Groups 1 and 2**); the establishment of Hamid Karzai as head of state in Afghanistan in June 2002 (separating **Groups 2 and 3**); and the capture of Saddam Hussein in Iraq in December 2003 (separating **Groups 3 and 4**). **Group 1** ends with Jack in recovery mode. External events bring back combat nightmares in **Groups 2 and 3**. **Group 4** signals a return to recovery mode. The chapter illustrates the process of recovery, exacerbation, and recovery again, which can happen in severe PTSD.
2. Jack's involvement as a speaker and leader in Overeaters Anonymous (OA) illustrates the process of redemption that may be possible for someone suffering from guilt dreams. Jack made use of his Roman Catholic faith in the form of the confession sacrament provided by the Church. Jack suffered from "moral injury," as did all of the other Vietnam veterans described in this book (Tom, Carlos, Andre, and Gary).

SEVEN

Explosion: Dream Revision for Triggered Memories

During the same period that I was meeting with veterans Tom, Andre, Gary, and Jack, between the years 2000 and 2007, I was also seeing nonmilitary patients from the San Diego community, some of whom were also suffering from PTSD. A rich source of PTSD patients from the civilian community was the State of California's workers compensation system, with whom I was licensed as a Certified Medical Evaluator. In this capacity I received referrals from employers for evaluation and treatment of their employees who had suffered work-related psychiatric injuries, some of which were severe enough to meet diagnostic criteria for PTSD. The patients presented in Chapters 7–9 (Luis, Kelly, and Bret) all had PTSD from workplace events. The patient presented in Chapter 10 (Cindy), for comparison with the others, had an adjustment disorder from stress experienced in the workplace. All patients were treated using dream revision techniques, and all showed substantial improvement. Their stories illustrate that dream revision, which I learned and perfected in relation to military combat trauma, could also be used effectively in civilian workplace settings.

Luis was born and raised in Durango, Mexico, the fourth of 11 children, with 2 brothers and 8 sisters. The family moved to California when he was in his teens. His 3 older siblings were out of the household from his early childhood, so he grew up as the oldest of the younger children. He told me, "I was always a loner." He graduated from high school in Riverside and went to work with his father in roofing.

He then worked in a variety of jobs over a 15-year period, including dishwasher, cook, automobile mechanic, and carwash operator. At that point he returned to roofing and had worked for the last three years with the same roofing company.

He married at age 20 and divorced at age 32. He had two children from this marriage, a 19-year-old daughter who lived in San Diego with her grandmother, and a 17-year-old son and girlfriend who lived in San Diego with Luis. Luis was in a common-law relationship with his own girlfriend who lived across the border in Tijuana, Mexico. Luis went there daily to see her. "She takes care of me" Luis told me, "we get along very well." Luis's parents also lived in Tijuana. His father was 82 with Alzheimer's Disease, "the same age and diagnosis as Ronald Reagan," Luis told me when we first met. Luis's mother was 72. He often stopped off to see his parents when he was in Tijuana to see his girlfriend.

In late August 1998, a propane gas tank exploded at Luis's worksite with the roofing company. Luis sustained severe burns, requiring emergency transfer by helicopter to the burn unit at the University of California, San Diego (UCSD) Hospital in San Diego. He spent seven weeks in UCSD Hospital, undergoing four plastic surgery procedures involving skin grafts. He received physical and occupational therapy as an outpatient at the hospital for an additional nine months.

In June 1999, 10 months after his injury, he began treatment with a bilingual (Spanish/English) psychiatrist at UCSD for PTSD. At that time Luis was having nightmares, flashbacks, severe anxiety, avoidance, irritability, decreased concentration, insomnia, crying spells, and depressed mood. The psychiatrist treated him with antidepressants, which may have helped, though Luis took them sporadically. The following year, in July 2000, Luis began supportive psychotherapy with a psychologist. In February 2001, two and a half years after the accident, Luis came to see me. He was 43 years old.

Luis received workers' compensation benefits, but was having trouble keeping doctors because he missed so many appointments. His lawyer came with him to the first session to assist in the process of getting started. Luis was 30 minutes late. While we waited for Luis, the lawyer told me that Luis was looking forward to having a "white" psychiatrist. I wasn't sure whether this was a good thing or a bad thing; it turned out to be a good thing.

When he did arrive, Luis was very distracted and anxious. He wanted to leave the office without being seen, but he stayed, his lawyer left, and I met with him alone. I got him to stay by having him talk about his girlfriend, whom he clearly cared about. He described vivid dreams and flashbacks. His concentration was poor; his descriptions of his family history and his injury at work were disjointed. Somehow we managed to get through the session.

As Luis explained to me, "My girlfriend and I sleep with pillows between us so I won't hurt her when I have a violent nightmare. Many of my nightmares involve fire. The burn injury gives me signaling problems in my brain, so I don't know when to stop eating, stop working, or move my bowels."

Luis was my patient for six years, from 2001 to 2007. During this period I met with him more or less monthly; he often missed appointments, saying he had forgotten or fallen asleep on the trolley. I did my best to accommodate his somewhat inconsistent lifestyle, which I attributed to his illness. In fact, he was a loyal and dependable patient, and we got along well. It probably helped that I was sympathetic regarding the severity of his injury and his resilience in being able to rebuild his life after such a trauma.

Over the years that I worked with Luis I tried him on a variety of antidepressants and other medications. Over time I was able to find some medications that reduced his anxiety, insomnia, and depression.

In addition to seeing me, Luis saw an internist for intestinal irritability. He had intermittent difficulties with swallowing, which he described as an "apple" in his throat, and occasional right-sided lower abdominal pain. Both of these symptoms seemed to get worse with stress. Luis continued to see his psychologist for supportive psychotherapy.

Luis shared 10 dreams with me over five and a half years:

Dream 1: 09/20/01 9/11 in the World Trade Center

I'm in the World Trade Center in New York City when the plane crashes into it. I get burned in the flames.

Dream 2: 09/20/01 9/11 in the Plane

I'm in a plane that crashes into the World Trade Center.

The World Trade Center bombings on September 11, 2001, served as a trigger to bring back memories, flashbacks, and nightmares of Luis's experience with the propane explosion roughly three years earlier (late August 1998). After Dream 1 he said, "I want to go to New York to comfort the people who were burned." After awakening from Dream 2 he said, "I knew it was a dream, since I've never been on an airplane in my life." He found the two dreams therapeutic in that after having them he could eat warm food, even hot chocolate, for the first time. He was very happy about this development.

As further therapy, I suggested he write a letter (in Spanish, his first language) to the burn victims from the World Trade Center bombings. I gave him the address of New York Hospital, Cornell Medical Center, Burn Unit, New York, N.Y. I assured him they would find someone at the hospital who could translate his letter into English.

Dream 3: 8/28/03 Arms Melting

My arms are melting with fire, like ice cream in the sun. I'm back in the helicopter, heading toward the hospital.

He said Dream 3 was triggered by a hearing a helicopter flying over his house, reminding him of the helicopter that brought him to UCSD Hospital. The fever caused by a recent liver infection might have been a factor as well. A third factor might have been the upcoming fifth anniversary date (8/31) of his original injury in 1998.

Dream 4: 9/18/03 Helicopter on Fire

I'm in a helicopter which is on fire. We are flying from Escondido to the University of California, San Diego (UCSD) Medical Center. As soon as we arrive at UCSD there is no fire. When I wake up, my arms are melting. The skin feels tender when I touch it.

Dream 4 was likely triggered by the fifth anniversary of his work injury (8/31/98), plus the second anniversary of the World Trade Center bombings (9/11/01). He told me he wrote a letter to the patients in New York City, but didn't know if they had received it. He said it felt good to write the letter, in any case.

After this dream, since I was concerned that a burning helicopter could develop into a recurrent dream for him, I introduced dream revision therapy for the first time in our treatment, suggesting the following revised dream:

There is a cord (chain) hanging down from the ceiling of the helicopter. Pulling the chain turns on the plane's (imaginary) sprinkler system, putting out the fire.

Luis indicated he would practice the revision, including pulling on the chain to put out the fire. He would tell the new dream to his girlfriend.

Dream 5: 9/18/03 Burning House (1)

My house is burning. I'm looking for a fire extinguisher. I'm trying to run away, but I have to wait for my friend. I wake up sweating; I peed in my bed.

The revision for Dream 4 could also work for Dream 5, since pulling on a chain or cord is simpler than searching for a fire extinguisher. I also suggested a second revision for Dream 5: that he looks ahead and sees his friend in a safe place. Luis liked this second revision, smiling when he heard it. He said he would rehearse it.

Dream 6: 04/24/04 Burning House (2)

My house is on fire. I wake up feeling relieved to see that it is OK.

After waking from Dream 6, Luis noted they had only one fire extinguisher at home. Following his girlfriend's suggestion, he bought a second fire extinguisher. This action helped relieve his anxiety. He was beginning to realize the principle of taking action, both in one's dreams and during wakefulness. He felt less like a victim, more like a resourceful survivor.

Dream 7: 03/03/05 Tsunami Wave

A tsunami wave comes over Chula Vista (a San Diego suburb, fronting on the harbor), but it is lava rather than just water. Hot water and lava all over. I get up, then go back to bed and dream about Madonna.

Dream 7 was triggered in part by the earthquake in Indonesia on 12/26/04, just over two months earlier. The earthquake and following tsunami wave caused the deaths of 230,000 people in areas around the Indian Ocean. Luis's dream converts the tsunami's ocean water into hot lava from a volcanic eruption, perhaps referring to Mt. Krakatoa, a volcano in Indonesia whose eruption in 1883 killed 40,000 people and spewed volcanic ash all around the globe for many months. In Dream 7 Luis has learned to take care of himself. He dreams about Madonna as a way of relaxing. He said "I enjoy listening to her singing." He told me his nightmare frequency had now decreased substantially. This was his first nightmare in five months, versus a previous frequency of two to three nightmares per month.

Dream 8: 09/08/05 Boiling Water

There is a metal bucket on the stove, with boiling water in it. My medications are put in the water. Workers compensation is not giving me medicine anymore. My feet are burning also.

Dream 8 was triggered by Luis's difficulty in getting one of his other doctor's prescriptions filled by his workers' compensation insurance company.

Dream 9: 01/05/06 Molten Spiderweb

There is a spiderweb in my room. A spider is holding the spiderweb with fire; drops come down from the web, like volcano lava. The spider never dies with the fire. I'm trapped with the spiderweb. My girlfriend woke me up. I woke up crying.

Dream 9 may have been triggered by the flu with a high fever. Luis said he tended to dream about his work injury when he got a fever. He said Dream 9 was a one-time dream which had not come back.

Dream 10: 03/27/07 Raining on the Roof

It's raining and raining. I am on the roof. The water tries to take me away, but it never does. I'm all by myself. I wake up sweating. It's a nightmare.

Luis reported Dream 10 at our last session. A dream about raining on a roof seems therapeutic in the sense that he had been working as a roofer when the explosion occurred. Rain is a good antidote to fire.

Luis told me that the day of our last session was his birthday. Five months earlier his girlfriend had given birth to a new baby girl. He was enjoying his five-month-old daughter very much and had the feeling his girlfriend was going to tell him on his birthday that she was pregnant again. Over the six years that we had worked together, Luis had come a long way toward full recovery from his serious psychological work injury.

TIPS FOR DREAM REVISION FROM CHAPTER 7

1. Current world events (and their anniversaries) can trigger nightmares related to an earlier trauma (as we saw earlier with Andre in Chapter 5 and Jack in Chapter 6). Luis' Dream 1 (9/11 in the World Trade Center) and Dream 2 (9/11 in the Plane) were triggered by the World Trade Center Bombings in New York City on 9/11/01. His Dream 3 (Arms Melting), Dream 4 (Helicopter on Fire), and Dream 5 (Burning House I) were most likely anniversary dreams related to his personal trauma on 8/31/98 and the World Trade Center bombings on 9/11/01. His Dream 7 (Tsunami Wave) was probably triggered by the earthquake in Indonesia on 12/26/04 that led to the deaths of 230,000 people.
2. It is helpful for patients, caregivers, and treaters all to be aware of such connections between world events (and anniversaries) and the exacerbation of PTSD symptoms.

EIGHT

Car Crash: Dream Revision for Adult and Child Trauma

Kelly arrived on time for her first interview, casually and attractively dressed in a stylish curve-fitting top with jeans. Her husband came with her and stayed in the waiting room. Kelly worked as a San Diego police officer and appeared bright and articulate, describing her situation calmly and clearly.

She had been off work for several weeks. Prior to that, she had felt anxious, sweaty, and nauseous. She lost her appetite, couldn't fall asleep at night, and—when she finally fell asleep—woke up with nightmares. She saw a psychiatrist who diagnosed her with work-related stress and put her on temporary disability leave. The police department referred her to me, as I had experience treating work stress in police officers.

Kelly attributed her symptoms to an incident that had occurred five months earlier. She had been working as a police officer on patrol duty in the City of San Diego for four years—sometimes alone, sometimes with another officer. On the date in question, she had been alone on the night shift. She got a call at 3 a.m. from her dispatcher. Someone had phoned 911 from the downtown area. There was a disturbance in a neighborhood building, where a person—having broken into a store—was trashing the place and making a loud racket.

Kelly's patrol car arrived on the scene before any others. She stopped her car, got out, and approached the store. Shattered pieces of glass were all over the sidewalk; the front of the store was wide open to the outside. Inside the store she could see a large man, about six feet tall, 180 pounds, appearing strong and muscular, and clearly drunk. He called her foul names (bitch, fucking bitch, cunt), and said he would kill her and everyone else. As she approached the store, he came after her, wielding a stick over his head.

Kelly drew her gun, her finger on the trigger, but restrained herself as the man swung at her with the stick and missed. She chased him down, handcuffed him, and took him into custody. At this point another police officer arrived on the scene to help her.

As it turned out, the drunken man with the stick had vandalized several other stores besides the one she found him in. He was an active-duty U.S. Marine, in training to be a military policeman, and his superiors intervened in the legal proceedings. He was charged only with vandalism and allowed to continue his military education.

Kelly felt frustrated, angry, and scared, annoyed at the unfairness of the legal system. She felt vulnerable to another attack, with this man still on the loose. He had not been punished, and she was now on disability leave, unable to work because of her extreme stress. She questioned her actions during the 3 a.m. encounter, wondering why she hadn't shot or killed him, which might have created a safer outcome, as other officers advised her.

She had also failed to shoot a violent methamphetamine-intoxicated man with schizophrenia who had confronted her in a similar incident several nights earlier. Other police officers told her not to be afraid to fire her weapon. She wondered whether she would be able to shoot someone if it became necessary.

My job as Kelly's treating psychiatrist was to find the cause of her stress—her anxiety, sweating, nausea, reduced appetite, difficulty sleeping, and nightmares—and to help her recover and return to work. Why was it so upsetting for her to arrest an intoxicated Marine at three o'clock in the morning?

Perhaps there were clues in her dreams. Early in the course of our treatment sessions, Kelly shared with me two dreams she had been having:

Dream 1: 08/05/02 Daughter Is Raped

My daughter is trying to call me. She has been raped. She is covered in blood. She is crying and screaming.

Dream 2: 08/05/02 Hands around my Neck

I'm going to a call. I get out of my police car. Someone comes after me. They put their hands around my neck. I'm trying to scream, get air.

Dream 2 is clearly about the 3 a.m. incident with the Marine in downtown San Diego. In order to understand Dream 1 more fully, I needed to know more about Kelly's background history before she became a police officer.

Kelly was born in Southern California to a teenage mother who gave her up for adoption. Her adoptive family later moved out of state. Her adoptive mother died when Kelly was three. Her adoptive father then went away and remarried, and Kelly and her three adoptive siblings had to live with relatives and in foster homes. Kelly was physically, verbally, and sexually abused during this period of time. Though reluctant to tell me about her childhood at first, later in therapy she shared the specific details.

Kelly married at age 17 and dropped out of high school. She had two children—a daughter now 14 and a son now 6—from that marriage, which lasted four years. While she told me she was too young to get married at such a young age, she seemed reluctant to disclose further details about the marriage. After her divorce she returned to California and met her birth mother, with whom she became close friends.

Back in California, Kelly finished her high school training, worked briefly as a medical assistant, and then decided to attend the police academy. Upon her graduation from the police academy, the San Diego Police Department had hired her as a patrol officer four years ago. Two years ago she married her present husband, also a San Diego police officer. They each had children from previous marriages, all combined together into a blended family. Kelly expressed satisfaction with her present marriage.

Dream 1—which seems to be about Kelly's daughter—is probably about both Kelly and her daughter. At the time Kelly experienced problems parenting her daughter, who became a runaway several months after this dream. Kelly's childhood history of sexual molestation suggests the dream may be about Kelly herself as well. Kelly reported both Dreams 1 and 2 to me at the same session on 08/05/02, suggesting they had occurred in close proximity to each other and were associated in her mind.

The man calling her foul names at 3 a.m., and coming after her with a stick held over his head, brought back memories of childhood scenes when she was small and vulnerable. Fortunately, she was now fully grown, and—through her own efforts—no longer vulnerable. As a policewoman, she was able to fend off her 3 a.m. attacker, handcuff him by herself, and bring him to the police station. Unfortunately, the drunken Marine did not receive adequate punishment for his 3 a.m. vandalism, providing a further reminder of childhood experiences, when a series of perpetrators went unpunished.

At this early phase in her treatment with me, Kelly was not interested in discussing her childhood, and I did not insist on it. She saw me regarding a work injury and wanted to return to work as soon as possible. I chose to let sleeping dogs lie, since this is what Kelly wanted. We could revisit the topic later if and when we needed to. I didn't understand the connection between Dreams 1 and 2 at the time she told them to me. Their full meaning only became apparent later, as we worked on other dreams together.

Kelly was 34 years old when she first came to see me in July 2002. I diagnosed her with PTSD and elected to treat her conservatively, since within several sessions she seemed to be recovering from the 3 a.m. incident. I prescribed medication for sleep and anxiety, and worked together with Kelly's therapist at getting Kelly to respect her own on-the-job decision-making capability. She had conducted herself well despite other people's second-guessing her.

Kelly recovered with supportive treatment and returned to work at full duty within four months of my first meeting with her. She continued to do well—at work and at home—over the next year until the occurrence of another traumatizing work-related event—a drunk driver ran a red light and hit her squad car, resulting in several injuries to Kelly and the totaling of her squad car. The most serious injury was to Kelly's neck, which ended up requiring fusion surgery of two cervical vertebrae. Prior to the spinal surgery she underwent a hysterectomy with bilateral oophorectomy (removal of her ovaries), making her suddenly menopausal at age 36.

Kelly went through a period of emotional deterioration following the accident and the two surgeries. The accident reactivated her PTSD and she became depressed. I treated her with medications for depression, anxiety, and insomnia. Nearly a year after her injury in the car accident, Kelly told me about the following recurrent nightmare she had started having:

Dream 3: 08/16/04 Air Bags Deployed

I'm trapped inside my patrol car and can't get help. I feel it is on fire. I can smell the deployed air bags. The equipment doesn't work. No one knows where I'm at.

When Kelly had this dream, she awoke feeling panicked, covered in sweat. Sometimes she got up for a while, went back to sleep, and reentered the dream. She felt extremely frustrated that she could not get out of the car.

In working with Kelly on Dream 3, I first helped clarify the actual details of her situation: 1) the car was not on fire; what seemed like smoke was powder from the air bags; 2) the air bags did deploy, preventing more serious—possibly life-threatening—injuries from occurring; 3) though the car's equipment wasn't working, she had her radio, which worked; 4) hindsight allowed us to confirm that she recovered from the accident, despite some (serious) injuries.

Using dream revision therapy, I encouraged Kelly to radio for help in her dream, which soon arrives and gets her out safely. She smiled as we discussed using her radio. This empowered her.

At the scene of the actual accident, some people in the neighborhood had called 911, and the firemen had come and got her out. Dream revision regarding the use of her radio helped reduce Kelly's feelings of helplessness and worthlessness during and after the accident. She agreed to rehearse the new dream, tell it to her husband and her girlfriends, and see what happened.

Just 10 days after our dream revision session with Dream 3, Kelly had the following dream:

Dream 4: 08/26/04 Outside My Car

I'm outside the car now, breathing easier, feeling better. I can see myself still inside the car as well.

Dream 4 shows that the dream revision method works. After sharing Dream 4 with me, Kelly told me she stopped having Dream 3 for a long time. She did have it again three years later, shortly before we were scheduled to end our sessions together:

Dream 16: 04/17/07 Trapped in Car

Trapped in a car, full of smoke, like it was on fire.

At the time of Dream 16 I reminded Kelly that three years earlier we had come up with a successful method for dealing with this nightmare, using her radio to call for assistance. Now, with all she had learned about dream revision, she might be able to do even better than before, getting the firemen to open the door from the outside, and using her own (dream) tools to open the door from the inside. Whatever help she needs is available; she has only to ask for it.

I saw Kelly only one more time, in May 2007, about a month after Dream 16, so I did not learn whether Dream 16 had permanently gone away. It feels unprofessional to me to contact patients about dream recurrences after our treatment is completed, so I do not do it, though I am happy to speak with, or write to, them if they contact me.

Following her initial neck surgery, Kelly experienced disabling neck pain, and underwent two subsequent surgical procedures, one for removal of hardware from the original surgery, and a second for radiofrequency treatment of nerve endings in her cervical spine. Her neck injury was too severe to allow her to continue working out of a squad car, a job requiring more physical agility than she now possessed. I had been talking with Kelly about looking for other ways of utilizing her significant skills. In this context, she presented me with three dreams at the same session:

Dream 5: 11/23/04 Comedy of Errors (I)

I go to work. I'm looking for a patrol car. I can't find the keys to the car. I go inside and ask for a key. I'm looking for my uniforms. I can't find my gun belt. I try to go out. I'm in the patrol car, but I have my tennis shoes on. I lock myself out of the car. Nothing is going right. I'm feeling frustrated, desperate.

Dream 6: 11/23/04 Comedy of Errors (II)

I'm going to a call, but I can't find the address. I'm not in my patrol car, but in my regular car. I say to the dispatcher, "Can you send somebody else?"

Dream 7: 11/23/04 Can't Go Back to Work

I come to see you (Dr. Dow). You tell me that I can't go back to work.

Dreams 5, 6, and 7 are all related to the same issue, that she can't go back to work. She struggles with her denial over this inconvenient truth. The dreams reflect her grieving over the loss of her job, going through the five grief stages: 1) denial and isolation, 2) anger, 3) bargaining, 4) depression, and 5) acceptance.[1] She seems to be in stages 1 and 2. This is real "dream work",[2] helping Kelly adjust to her new situation. Kelly's dreams are telling her something: she cannot return to her job as a patrol officer, no matter how hard she tries. It is a good sign her dreams are changing. She is no longer stuck, like a broken record. She is moving forward in her dreams and hopefully in her life.

Two months later she reported the following dream.

Dream 8: 01/25/05 Government Agent

I'm working as an agent in the government. I'm chasing people, getting shot at, with bullets, missiles. There are different versions (in the snow, in my car, in the mall). I wake up drenched in sweat, with my heart racing.

The changing versions of Dream 8 are a good sign. Dream 8 qualifies as a nightmare, in that she wakes up sweating, with her heart racing, but it comes in different flavors, indicating that her dreaming mechanisms are not completely paralyzed. She is starting to adjust to the prospect of giving up her patrol officer career, but still clings to it, both during wakefulness and in her dreams.

A few months after Dream 8, Kelly had a series of dreams about women and children, including herself.

Dream 9: 03/01/05 Chased by Snake

A huge snake is chasing me. A lady says, "Your picture is in a book for prostitutes." For awhile I can hide from it. I get to my apartment. I'm looking for my clothes, so I can move out. I can't find a bag to put my clothes in. A lady says, "Find a river rock to kill the snake." I go out behind the building where I live. I'm wrestling with the snake. I hit it with a rock. Its head comes off; the body is chasing me. Everyone is going on with their normal life. I have nothing with me but a jacket and a pair of pants. I wake up covered with sweat.

Dream 10: 03/01/05 Handsome Man

I see a tall, dark, handsome man in my dreams. I am always trying to be with him. All these things are obstacles, stopping me.

Dream 9 is a recurrent dream: "It comes in many variants," Kelly told me, "including helicopters, ocean, the drowning of my beloved dog." Snake dreams are often sexual.[3] Kelly said she had been sexually abused by men when she was a child. Dream 9 is about confronting her abuser(s) and not trying to run away from them. Kelly became a policewoman as a strategy of self-protection, whether consciously or unconsciously. It proved to be a highly successful strategy, but now her neck injury had become career ending. This created a great deal of stress for Kelly. Her new traumas brought back PTSD symptoms related to past traumas from childhood. This phenomenon is known as "the black hole of PTSD."[4] Each new trauma sucks all the old ones into it. Such piling up of traumas makes the new trauma all the more difficult to deal with.

Fortunately, Kelly was learning how to deal effectively with the new traumas, preparing her to deal with the older traumas from her childhood. This provided a huge opportunity for our therapy. Finally, Kelly was willing to talk with me about her childhood. The dream gave her permission.

The man in Dream 10 could be Kelly's present husband, whom she trusts. As can be seen from the dates, Kelly shared Dreams 9 and 10 with me on the same day. Combining the two dreams, I suggested that I was in alliance with the man in Dream 10. I advised Kelly to use a more effective weapon against the snake in Dream 9; this is different from the woman's advice in the dream. A rock is not the best way to kill a snake. A machete might be better, or perhaps her service pistol. I told her she had the power in her dream to call for any weapon she wanted. She also had the power to direct the weapon accurately at any part of the snake she wished to hit.

I was aware of the sexual implications in Kelly's snake dream, but chose to stay within the dream and its snake metaphor. Why expose her unnecessarily to unpleasant childhood traumas at this point, and possibly risk triggering feelings of helplessness and hopelessness? There was no need to look further. We had the means of getting rid of the snake itself without pursuing its possible symbolic meanings. As a patrol officer—in her dreams if no longer in her waking life—Kelly could deal with a snake.

Dream 11: 03/01/05 Overhead Compartment

I'm on a plane. I can't find my kid. He's up in this overhead compartment.

Dream 12: 04/19/05 Dead Man in River

I am with my sister, in Idaho where she lives, at the edge of a river. She is a police officer. I am an ex-police officer. We see two wires in the river. We get the idea to use the wires to plug in our dryers to blow-dry our hair. As we pull on the wires, we discover that one of them has a man's dead body on it. I want to check out the body to see how the man died (bullet holes, blunt trauma, etc.). My sister is freaked out, grossed out by the body, and won't have anything to do with it. We argue over this (i.e., what you need to do to be a good police officer). Then the body crawls back into the water. At this point I wake up.

Kelly told me at the time of Dream 12 that the snake dreams (which had been recurrent for years) were gone. She speculated that perhaps she had found a weapon that got rid of the snake. None of Kelly's dreams over the next two years included any actual snakes (though there may have been some metaphorical ones). As we proceeded through her dreams, Kelly showed signs of successfully processing her childhood traumas.

In Dream 12 Kelly tries to make her sister into a police officer, but it doesn't work. Kelly didn't fully explain this to me after Dream 12, but she opened up more after Dream 14, which we shall address shortly.

Dream 13: 06/17/05 Wedding Hotel

I'm frantic. I'm trying to go to a wedding with my friend, my best girlfriend. We're staying in a hotel. Every floor when we get off the elevator, something different is there. We can never find the floor we need to go to. I'm sweating, feeling out of control. I can't wake up from the dream. Each time I go back to bed, I go back into the dream.

Dream 13 is about Kelly's female friend who thinks her husband is having an affair. The hotel search may be an effort to catch her friend's husband in bed with his lover. Kelly is frustrated by her friend's lack of assertiveness in confronting her husband. In a sense, Dream 13 is a companion to Dream 12. Kelly is trying to teach assertiveness to other women she cares about, but her efforts are not successful.

Dream 14: 06/28/05 Dead Kids

My kids are dead. My grandfather killed them when I wouldn't have sex with him.

Dreams 11 and 14 are anxiety dreams about her children (as was Dream 1). Kelly told me at the time of Dream 14 that her grandfather molested her from age 6 to 10. She was later molested in a series of foster homes until she got married at age 17, which stopped the molestations. Her recent traumas brought back memories of her childhood molestations, and she wanted to protect her children from what happened to her.

As dream revision therapy for these dreams about her children, I proposed that she hire a police guard (a "dream" guard) to watch over her children, especially at night while they sleep. She liked this idea, and agreed to rehearse it.

I pointed out that her ongoing neck pain contributed to her nightmares. Medical treatment of the neck pain might help relieve the nightmares, by taking away the stimulus (trigger) for painful memories.

Kelly also told me at the time of Dream 14 that her grandfather molested her sister as well as Kelly. Her grandfather never got punished for his actions, and is now dead. In revisiting Dream 12 after she revealed these facts, we wondered whether the dead man in that dream might be her grandfather. She found this thought comforting; at least her grandfather got punished in her dreams. Unfortunately, as Dream 12 suggests, Kelly's sister has not managed to recover the way Kelly has.

Dream 15: 08/01/05 Can't Save Anyone

I'm trying to save people (especially women), but I can't do it. I feel helpless because I can't help anybody else.

Dream 15 recalls many other dreams in the series (Dreams 1, 11, and 14 about her children; Dreams 12 and 13 about her sister and her female friend). Kelly's motive for becoming a police officer included protecting others (especially women and children) as well as herself. In relation to Dream 15, I pointed out to Kelly that despite her work injury, she could still help battered women in some way if she chose to. She said she would think about this.

The last of Kelly's 17 dreams in the present series took place shortly before our last session:

Dream 17: 04/17/07 Pool Fish

My kids are in the pool. A big fish is nipping at them, with big teeth. I call out to them, "Get out of the pool!" We're standing at the pool deck. We run down the open deck. My daughter has just used heroin. Her boyfriend is standing there.

My suggestion regarding Dream 17 was that Kelly get help for her daughter. I provided Kelly with the names of possible treaters. Kelly's daughter—age 19 at the time of this dream—was not using heroin, but marijuana, alcohol, and prescription painkillers, including some of Kelly's. Kelly felt concerned in this dream that her daughter's drug and alcohol abuse might lead her to become a heroin junkie.

At the time of our last session in May 2007, Kelly had recovered substantially from her physical injuries and emotional trauma. Due to her neck injury, she was no longer able to work as a patrol officer and was planning to retire from the police department.

In the meantime, she had become a celebrity. She developed a new line of SWAT team clothing, especially for women, but also for men, and a local TV news program featured her line. Her husband helped her set up this new business. Her husband joined her for our last session, as I was closing my San Diego practice and moving to Boston. They seemed quite happy together; his support provided valuable stability for her.

Kelly gave me a Navy-blue hooded SWAT-team sweatshirt as a going-away gift. I put it on over my shirt and tie, and we had a big goodbye hug. We were both understandably proud of the progress we had made in helping her recover from PTSD, which could continue to help her face the big life changes ahead of her, as she switched careers and continued parenting her four children.

TIPS FOR DREAM REVISION FROM CHAPTER 8

1. Adult trauma can reawaken childhood trauma; effective therapy must deal with all traumas, past and present.
2. The pain from an injury (Kelly's neck injury) can serve as an ongoing reminder of the trauma that caused the injury, and thus trigger PTSD symptoms. Obtaining effective medical treatment for the injury is important in PTSD recovery.
3. If a recurrent nightmare seems metaphorical, as in the case of Kelly's Dream 9 (Chased by Snake), it is easiest and most effective to conduct dream revision within the metaphor. In revising a metaphorical dream, one focuses on the dreamer's emotion: how do they feel in the dream, and how would they like to feel?

NINE

Junkyard Dog: Revising Dreams That Involve Guilt

Bret had been a San Diego County police officer for 12 years when I first met with him in my office in January 2001. He was 35 years old, Caucasian, single, tall, and muscular. His large right hand felt strong and forceful when we shook hands for the first time. He was tense and obviously stressed, but friendly. He told me he was feeling angry and irritable, having trouble sleeping, waking up with nightmares. He was working, but felt he could no longer carry out his duties as a deputy sheriff. He felt he needed to take some time off from work.

About a year before our first meeting, Bret had shot and killed a bank robber at close range. Bret was at work on patrol duty at the time. He and his partner had been called to the scene following a report that a bank robbery had taken place, with the robber escaping on foot to a nearby residential neighborhood. Bret's partner found the suspect first and exchanged fire with him. Bret came upon the scene a short time later. He first noticed the suspect lying on the ground covered in blood, a gun still in his hand but pointed off to the side. Bret's partner was nearby, white as a sheet, saying "I'm out." Bret thought his partner meant he had been shot; as it turned out, he was not shot but had pulled a muscle in his leg and was unable to stand. The suspect lifted his gun and pointed it at Bret, saying, "Kill me! Kill me!" Bret fired five times until the suspect fell backward. Bret rushed up and placed handcuffs on the suspect, who by this time was already dead. Later, Bret learned that the bank robber was facing a long mandatory jail sentence without chance of parole, and may have chosen to be killed rather than go to prison.

Within several days of the shooting, Bret became agitated and irritable, "pumped up with adrenaline." He took three weeks off from work and saw a counselor, but didn't feel comfortable with her. He said, "She seemed less interested in me than in her own expertise." He stopped the counseling and returned to work.

Over the next year Bret felt increasingly burned out at work. "For the past six months," he told me, "I had to drag myself to work." He noticed himself becoming more emotional. Watching violence on television triggered his emotions. His sleep deteriorated and became fragmented. He had vivid unpleasant dreams several times per week. He developed a recurrent nightmare of a maze of overpasses going on forever, surrounded by people who wanted to do him harm. Sometimes he awakened out of a sound sleep with his heart racing, breathing hard, but without being able to recall any dream. Other times he woke up crying without knowing why. He rarely had daytime flashbacks. Some colleagues in the police department noticed his emotional stress and irritability and recommended he see a counselor. The police department sent him to me.

I put Bret on temporary disability leave and started him on medication for depression, anxiety, and insomnia. I encouraged him to talk about the shooting and agreed to see him regularly and frequently. As our meetings got under way, he reported having flashbacks about the killing scene and began sharing his nightmares with me. He was very interested in his nightmares; he wanted to know what they meant. We agreed to focus the therapy sessions on his dreams; he would do his best to remember dreams so we would have material to discuss.

Regarding the shooting episode, he told me he was initially proud of what he had done, but later felt bad about it; he felt bad about feeling proud. He was treated like a hero by his fellow police officers, so the bad feelings were internal. He felt bad that the bank robber was just a young man and had come from a good family. Bret wondered about changing careers, getting more education, and perhaps becoming a drug counselor. Later he indicated he might like to study psychology and learn more about PTSD.

Bret was born in San Diego, the older of two sons. Bret's father was in the Air Force and the family lived all over the country, which Bret felt was disruptive to his childhood. He finished high school near Baltimore and joined the Army, where he spent three years in the airborne infantry, jumping out of airplanes more than 30 times. His military service did not include involvement in combat.

He moved to San Diego in 1987 at age 21, joined the reserves, attended community college for a few semesters, and enrolled in the police academy. On the police force for 12 years and on patrol duty for 8 years, he had been dedicated to his work, receiving many awards and difficult dangerous assignments, but was frustrated that he wasn't moving forward in the department. Other people, less qualified than he was, were moving ahead of him. He felt he was perhaps too frank, not politically correct enough. He described himself as the "junkyard dog." In recent months he had been assigned to the night shift, sleeping in the daytime. He had requested a different shift but was not able to get it.

His parents lived in a suburb of San Diego. Both were working, his father for a state agency, his mother with a local university. His father, a Vietnam veteran, had been a military policeman (MP) in the Air Force, protecting an air base from the Viet Cong and the North Vietnamese during the Tet Offensive. He had been treated for PTSD 10 years earlier with medication and psychotherapy, during a period when he and Bret's mother were having marital problems, which they subsequently resolved. Bret's father was now fully recovered from his earlier PTSD.

Bret's maternal grandparents also lived in the San Diego area. His grandfather had served in the Army in World War II as a combat medic, working as a litter jeep driver in the South Pacific (mostly New Guinea). He had developed PTSD from his military experiences during World War II, superimposed upon a traumatic incident at age 12 when he accidentally killed his 14-year-old brother while they were hunting together. Bret's grandfather still suffered from PTSD and alcoholism. As Bret told me, "I was the oldest of his nine grandchildren, the only one who stood up to him. He hasn't forgiven me for that. Though he lives just a few miles away, I haven't seen him in seven or eight years. I'm not afraid of him, but of myself, what I might say to him if he got me angry. Seven or eight years ago I was in my patrol car, late at night, driving a drunken Mexican to a local jail. The Mexican was yelling at me through the grill with his beer breath. I had a flashback of my grandfather yelling at me as a child. I was frozen at a traffic light for two cycles. I haven't seen my grandfather since then."

Bret lived alone and rented a condo. He had been in several serious relationships with women, including an engagement, but was not in a rush to get married. A relationship had just broken up several months before he came to see me. He was sexually active and did not want medications that might affect his sexual function. As our therapy proceeded, Bret declined to take either antidepressants or antianxiety medications out of concern for side effects (sexual dysfunction and addiction). For a brief time he did accept a sleeping pill to help with insomnia.

BRET'S DREAMS

Over the entire course of our nearly five years of therapy together (January 2001 to December 2005), Bret shared a total of 46 dreams with me. The dreams, dates, titles, lengths, and themes are shown in Table 9.1. In order to review these dreams in relation to important stages in Bret's therapy I have divided them into five groups. Dreams 1–13 constitute **Group 1 (Off Work)**, during the initial 12 months of his therapy with me, starting on 01/29/01. On 02/04/02 Bret was able to return to work at "restricted duty" (desk job). Dreams 14–17 constitute **Group 2 (Restricted Duty)**, starting after he began restricted duty and continuing up to his advance to "public contact" on 07/08/02, a total of 5 months. Dreams 18–30 constitute **Group 3 (Public Contact)**, beginning with the onset of public contact, and continuing up to his advance to "suspect contact" on 01/09/03, a total of 6 months. Dreams 31–40 constitute **Group 4 (Suspect Contact)**, beginning with the onset of suspect contact, and continuing up to his work level advance to "full duty" on 9/12/03, a total of 8 months. Dreams 41–46

Table 9.1 Dreams in a Policeman with PTSD

#	Date	Dream Title	Lines	Theme
1	01/29/01	overpasses	2	being chased
3		watching torture	1	torture
4	04/24/01	vaccine cure	3	being chased
5		Viking boat	2	being chased
6		loose change	2	frustration
7	05/10/01	wadded up bills	6	frustration
8	05/24/01	stolen van	8	success
9	08/02/01	spaceship tidal wave	6	being chased
10	08/16/01	line of girls	2	woman
11	09/13/01	pro football team	2	neutral
12		boxer in the ring	3	being chased
13	10/09/01	yelling grandfather	2	displeased
14	02/14/02	my friends walk away	3	rejected

15	04/12/02	vindicated in court	4	success
16	05/10/02	mansion biker party	7	destruction
17		undercover cop	11	being chased
18	07/29/02	nasty nurse & pliers	9	woman
19		Chinese woman	1	woman
20	08/12/02	Toll House cookies	1	neutral
21	09/10/02	junkyard dog	4	being chased
22	09/26/02	no privacy for sex	6	woman
23		sunlight sex	3	woman
24	10/10/02	shoulder massage	4	success
25		5-round gun	6	frustration
26	11/11/02	beat-up salesman	8	guilt
27		water bottle	1	frustration
28	01/09/03	shaving my head	6	success
29		hospital tidal wave	7	being chased/w
30		mutilated people	3	frustration
31	01/23/03	tidal wave stops	6	being chased/w
32		driving backward	7	frustration
33	02/06/03	great white shark	9	being chased
34	02/20/03	Las Vegas closet sex	6	woman
35	03/20/03	railroad crossing	7	being chased
36		folding laundry	5	frustration
37	04/10/03	skydiving scared	4	fear/w
38	07/31/03	boot camp weapon	8	frustration/w
39	08/14/03	crying WWII vets	3	frustration
40		cops getting killed	3	frustration
41	12/05/03	girl in Dave's RV	14	frustration/w
42	05/07/04	mean dog is killed	6	being chased
43		taking care of business	5	being chased
44	07/30/04	commando team in Norway	10	being chased/w
45	04/28/05	people out the window	4	killing
46	05/26/05	Pentagon assistants	10	woman

The "w" indicates dreams that include a woman in addition to other themes.

constitute **Group 5 (Full Duty)**, Bret's full duty dreams. Bret shared dreams with me for 20 months following his return to full duty. Taken as a whole, Bret's dreams document his stepwise improvement from serious impairment with PTSD to full recovery and return to patrol duty as a deputy sheriff.

Nearly a third of Bret's dreams (14 out of 46) involved BEING CHASED. The BEING CHASED dreams are listed separately in Table 9.2 and clustered according to Bret's work status into **Groups 1–5**. The five BEING CHASED dreams in **Group 1 (Off Work)** are presented below.

Table 9.2 Dreams of Being Chased (n=14)

#	Date	Dream Title/Work Level	Group	Months
	[01/29/01	**Work Level 1: Off Work]**		**12**
1	01/29/01	Overpasses	1	
4	04/24/01	Vaccine Cure	1	
5	04/24/01	Viking Boat	1	
9	08/02/01	Space Ship Tidal Wave	1	
12	09/13/01	Boxer in the Ring	1	
	[02/04/02	**Work Level 2: Restricted Duty]**		**5**
17	05/10/02	Undercover Cop*	2	
	[07/08/02	**Work Level 3: Public Contact]**		**6**
21	09/10/02	Junkyard Dog	3	
29	01/09/03	Hospital Tidal Wave	3	
	[01/09/03	**Work Level 4: Suspect Contact]**		**8**
31	01/23/03	Tidal Wave Stops	4	
33	02/06/03	Great White Shark	4	
35	03/20/03	Railroad Crossing	4	
	[09/12/03	**Work Level 5: Full Duty]**		**20**
42	05/07/04	Mean Dog Is Killed	5	
43	05/07/04	Taking Care of Business	5	
44	07/30/04	Commando Team in Norway	5	

*dream revision therapy training

Dream 1: 01/29/01 Overpasses

I am traveling on a maze of overpasses going on forever, surrounded by people that want to do me harm.

Dream 4: 04/24/01 Vaccine Cure

I'm in charge of a cure or a vaccine or something. People are trying to get it from me. I'm being chased. I want to use it for the good of everyone. They want to hide it.

Dream 5: 04/24/01 Viking Boat

I'm a Viking, on the boat, with the sword, the whole nine yards. People are trying to kill me. I'm being chased.

Dream 9: 08/02/01 Spaceship Tidal Wave

I'm the leader of a group of people leaving earth for a mission in outer space. Spaceships are taking off without me. A huge tidal wave is coming, pouring all over the land. Waves are 60–100 feet high. I am on a balcony. I see that I have to run to avoid getting hit by the wave. I am running through barbed wire and razor wire, jumping over deep holes. Everything is very vivid. Then I wake up.

Dream 12: 09/13/01 Boxer in the Ring

I'm a boxer in the ring, beating everybody. When I climb through the rope to get out of the ring, my life is a mess. The Mafia are chasing me; I have a crooked trainer; my wife is a bitch. Then I wake up.

In Dreams 1, 4, and 5 the pursuer is not specified except as "people." In Dream 9 the pursuer is a tidal wave. In Dream 12 the pursuer is the Mafia. The basic theme of these BEING CHASED dreams remains largely unchanged despite the change in content.

After Dreams 4 and 5, which were clearly different from Dream 1, his familiar BEING CHASED nightmare, Bret felt elated, "better than I've felt in years. I'm having almost religious thoughts about the shooting. It was meant that I would be there that day. I passed up an invitation to go to a wedding in LA with my girlfriend. It was a beautiful day. I asked for the assignment to that particular beach area, thinking it would be an easy day, eating, watching girls, etc. I had to pull rank to get a car; there weren't enough to go around. My car number turned out to be 211, the legal code for armed robbery (section 211). I needed to be there to help my partner out. I don't ever want to kill another human being if I don't have to, even though they gave me the Medal of Valor."

After Dream 12, Bret's fifth BEING CHASED dream in 8 months of therapy, I was gratified to see the changes in content, but concerned that the BEING CHASED theme was not going away. Recurrent nightmares tend to get increasingly repetitive over time, as had become apparent to me in working with Vietnam veterans (Chapters 1–6), whose traumas were more than 20 years in the past. My experience in treating PTSD patients has taught me not to let nightmares become too repetitive. When Luis (in Chapter 7) told me his burning helicopter nightmare and Kelly (in Chapter 8) told me her snake nightmare, I made a decision to teach each of them how to rescript a recurrent nightmare and thereby prevent its further recurrence.

In Bret's case, after hearing five BEING CHASED dreams, I decided to intervene with his next BEING CHASED dream, to see if dream revision techniques might work with Bret. Though still having BEING CHASED dreams, Bret was definitely making progress in therapy. On 02/04/02, after we had discussed and interpreted his first 13 dreams, he felt ready to return to work at restricted duty. Three months after beginning restricted duty, on 05/10/02, he finally had another BEING CHASED dream, the only one in **Group 2 (Restricted Duty)**.

Dream 17: 05/10/02 Undercover Cop

I'm an undercover cop, being chased by a bunch of people who are trying to kill me. I'm going through a warehouse or garage. There are lights only intermittently, with darkness in between. I'm being chased. There has been fighting and shooting. I run into a hallway. There is a glass partition, through which I can see another part of this warehouse or garage, but there is no way through the partition. Then I see a half door with a shelf (like a service opening for a parts department). I go through the opening, but it doesn't lead to the other side of the partition. Instead, I'm in a little room, a storage room, with tools, building equipment, oxygen tanks. There is no way out. I'm trapped. Then I wake up.

Dream 17 was very vivid and scary for Bret. In this dream he is pursued as an undercover cop by a bunch of people who are trying to kill him, and end up trapping him in a small storage room. He is only able to escape by waking up. For the first time in our therapy I informed Bret that he could change his BEING CHASED dream by rescripting it. Waking up is always a solution to a scary nightmare, but might there be a dream revision that would allow him to remain safe without waking up?

Bret welcomed this challenge as an opportunity. I proposed several possible changes: stronger weapons (automatic pistols, hand grenades, tear gas, mace) to fight off his pursuers; more police officers; a trap door and tunnel as an escape route. However, regarding the trap door and tunnel, continuing to run away is not the best option in a BEING CHASED dream; I advised Bret to stand his ground and confront his pursuers assertively, even aggressively if necessary. Bret got the idea. He chose to develop a strategy on his own. He would then rehearse it, go to sleep, and let me know the results.

Dream revision seemed to be helpful, because only two months after the dream revision session involving Dream 17, Bret felt ready to advance another work level to "public contact" on 07/08/02. Bret had two BEING CHASED dreams at this level which are included in **Group 3 (Public Contact)**.

Dream 21: 09/26/02 Junkyard Dog

A huge dog comes chasing after me, foaming at the mouth. It chases me through a junkyard, with car parts, debris, trash. I shoot the dog. An unidentified person asks me "Why did you kill my dog?" I wake up, feeling jacked up (i.e., excited) and angry.

Dream 29: 01/09/03 Hospital Tidal Wave

I'm the hotshot, hot-shit surgeon, badass doctor, like George Clooney. It's a high-rise hospital. A tidal wave has flooded the hospital. I have a stethoscope around my neck. The head of the stethoscope keeps falling off. All the nurses want to have sex with me, in broom closets, everywhere. I work my way up from floor to floor as the water rises, saving patients and having sex with nurses. I'm about ready to orgasm. Then I wake up.

In Dream 21 when the huge junkyard dog comes after him, foaming at the mouth, Bret shoots the dog. Finally, Bret has stopped running. He has used his gun to shoot his pursuer. Dream 21, appearing just four months after Dream 17, when Bret first learned about dream revision, is a key dream in the series. It has healing features: confronting the monster by killing it, not running away anymore. Dream 21 is the beginning of the end of Bret's BEING CHASED dreams.

Who or what does the dog in Dream 21 represent? In one sense the junkyard dog is Bret himself. This was his nickname, given to Bret by his colleagues long before Bret's shooting of the bank robber. He is "bad bad Leroy Brown, baddest man in the whole damn town . . . meaner than a junkyard dog."[1] The dog represents Bret's guilt over killing the bank robber. In order to stop running, he has to kill his guilt. In a sense, he has to kill his old self; killing the dog is killing the tough mean guy he used to be.

The dog is also the bank robber. Bret has to kill the bank robber a second time in order to be free of his nightmare. He killed the bank robber once in real life; now he kills the bank robber oneirically, in his dream. As we see later, Bret will need to kill the dog at least two more times before he can be free of it.

Bret began in therapy as macho and impulsive, a junkyard dog. I told him he reminded me of the early Clint Eastwood in the "spaghetti western" movies like *A Fistful of Dollars, For a Few Dollars More, The Good, the Bad, and the Ugly*: the "make my day" gunslinger ready to shoot first and ask questions later.

I proposed to Bret that he consider the later version of Clint Eastwood in such movies as *Unforgiven, In the Line of Fire, The Bridges of Madison County*, and *Million Dollar Baby*. In these movies Clint Eastwood is less macho, less explosive, more mature, and just as effective—if not more effective—than in the early movies.

Bret had a story of his own about male maturity, more explicitly sexual than my Clint Eastwood example: the story from the movie *Colors* about the old bull who doesn't chase cows all over the field, but just walks calmly down the hill to the herd, and chooses whichever cow he wants.[2]

Dream 29 is the Leroy Brown song and the old bull story fused together as a revised version of Bret's recurrent nightmare. The pursuer in a BEING CHASED dream has become a tidal wave, a common phenomenon in PTSD. Luis's Dream 7 (Tsunami Wave) in Chapter 3 was like this. In Bret's Dream 29 he has become the "hotshot, hot-shit, . . . badass doctor, like George Clooney," who played a sexy doctor in the television hospital drama, ER. As the tidal wave floods the hospital, Bret uses the wave like an elevator to climb from floor to floor, having sex with all the nurses along the way. In this sense the tidal wave represents Bret's rising sexual excitement. However, the tidal wave remains dangerous, so Bret wakes himself up in order to escape it, thereby forgoing his sexual climax.

On the date of Dream 29, 01/09/03, Bret moved up to the next work level, "suspect contact." He had three BEING CHASED dreams at this level, which are included in **Group 4 (Full Duty)**.

Dream 31: 01/23/03 Tidal Wave Stops

I'm in a hospital. A beautiful woman, Playboy centerfold type, is lying on a gurney, covered in blood, with tubes everywhere. A huge tidal wave is coming at us. A black book is floating on the tidal wave. I want the tidal wave to stop. Using my therapy training, I command it to stop, and it stops. It freezes in place. Then I wake up. I feel frustrated. I want to know what happens next.

Dream 33: 02/06/03 Great White Shark

I'm the leader of this group of people, trying to get them out of an old hospital or school building (circa 1920). The building has hardwood floors. People are behind me following me, also in front of me. I can't see any of their faces. On the right against the wall is a row of wooden benches without backs. A great white shark breaks through the hardwood floor. I jump on the bench to get off the floor, which becomes liquid. I can't stand on the bench, or else it would give way. I have to crawl on it. I need to get back on the floor, but then the shark comes.

Dream 35: 03/20/03 Railroad Crossing

I'm driving through a junkyard, like a desert terrain, moving real fast in a jeep. There are foothills, rocks, chaparral, dirt roads, there is junk everywhere. I'm being chased. I've got to negotiate through all this crap. I go over a ridge out of the junkyard, and it begins again. Finally, I realize I can control my dreams. I come to a railroad crossing with the signals down. Ding-ding-ding-ding.

The tidal wave theme, already present in Dreams 9 and 29, returns in Dream 31, now reflecting Bret's increasing mastery of dream revision. Like Moses parting the Red Sea, Bret orders the tidal wave to stop. It is interesting to speculate whether after Dreams 9 and 29 Bret specifically rehearsed getting the tidal wave to stop. If not, then his successful commanding of the tidal wave to stop in Dream 31 might make him a "lucid dreamer," a person who can change a dream spontaneously—from within the dream—without the necessity of rehearsing before going to sleep.[3]

In Dream 33 Bret's junkyard dog pursuer is replaced by a great white shark. The junkyard dog image came from the song about Leroy Brown, a large mean black man from Chicago. Bret is a large mean white man from San Diego. He has now found an image more appropriate to himself, a great white shark. This is a significant step toward healing, in the sense that Bret can now more easily appreciate that he is his own pursuer, both the one chasing and the one BEING CHASED.

Between Dreams 33 and 35, during our session of 03/06/03, Bret had an important insight: that he was using thrill-seeking as a means of controlling worry. We talked again about the young Clint Eastwood and the older Clint Eastwood, and the need for Bret to develop a more mellow, mature self.

In Dream 35 Bret is back in the junkyard of Dream 21, but with no dog in evidence. Bret once again shows he has control over his dreams. Despite BEING CHASED, he stops at a railroad crossing (ding-ding-ding-ding) and nothing happens to him. No need to run anymore; nothing to run from. The message of the train is to slow down, not overexert, not try to do more than he needs to. We discussed the movie, *Tin Cup*, in which the main character, played by Kevin Costner, repeatedly tries to get a hole in one and fails. The relevant golfing term is to "lay up": hit a shot that is good enough to win, not necessarily a perfect shot.

Six months after Dream 35, on 09/12/03, Bret was able to return to work at "full duty," a major achievement for a police officer who carries a gun and has to chase down criminals. Bret had three BEING CHASED dreams while back at **Full Duty (Group 5)**, but these dreams seem different from the earlier ones.

Dream 42: 05/07/04 Mean Dog Is Killed

I'm working as a deputy, with a group of people. The people are afraid of this big mean dog. No one will leave the patio. I say I'll handle the dog; I'm not afraid. But they won't let me. I wake up

I go back to sleep and the dream resumes. I'm on the porch again. Someone runs up and says that someone has just killed the dog. I wake up again. Time to get up.

Dream 43: 05/07/04 Taking Care of Business

This big huge dog is staring at me. People are behind me, screaming and yelling. The dog looks at me. He comes at me and tries to bite me. I shoot him in the head. People ask me how could I manage to do that? I say I was just taking care of business. Then I wake up.

Dream 44: 07/30/04 Commando Team in Norway

I'm the leader of a commando team. Everyone is looking at me to make sure the mission went well. Two other guys are with me. There is a beautiful blonde girl on the team. I'm the alpha male. I'm all over her, and she's all over me. We are running for our lives. Soldiers are coming after us. We are trying to blow up a heavy water plant in Norway (like in the movie with Kirk Douglas).

The scene shifts to a cabin, in the midst of snow-covered mountains, an idyllic, isolated setting. We have great sex. Then we do the mission. We blow up the plant. I'm hand in hand with the girl, running away. We get into a vehicle.

Dreams 42 and 43 involve the junkyard dog. In Dream 42 people are afraid of the dog. In Dream 43 Bret kills the dog once again: "just taking care of business." This is a recovery dream. Bret was just taking care of business when he killed the junkyard dog, just taking care of business when he killed the bank robber. Bret's father had to strangle a Vietcong woman at close range, as she was about to set off an explosive charge. Bret kills the dog at close range, just as he killed the bank robber. He is now at full capacity, no longer disabled. At the time of Dreams 42 and 43, Bret told me "Work is going well. I have a new style, more mellow than before. I'm happy about this." He seemed more confident in himself.

Dream 44 is also a recovery dream. Bret is a movie star again, not Clint Eastwood or George Clooney, but Kirk Douglas in *The Heroes of Telemark*. Bret is still BEING CHASED, but he is now a James Bond-like character with a sexy female companion. He and his team are heroes of the resistance movement in World War II, blowing up a Nazi heavy water plant in Norway. By enlisting a woman to run with him in Dream 44, Bret manages to elude his pursuers without having to relinquish his sexuality as in Dream 31.

After Dream 44 Bret said, "I saw the movie with Kirk Douglas. I have my act together, both work and women. I feel good about myself, have turned the corner. Life is too short to be Johnnie badass. I learned from the movie, *Tin Cup*, that you don't have to hit a hole in one every time." Our last session was in December 2005, seven months after Bret's last reported dream (Dream 46).

In the course of reviewing and analyzing Bret's dreams we have only dealt with his 14 BEING CHASED dreams. The other 32 dreams may be of interest in other contexts, but here I chose to focus on his BEING CHASED dreams, since those were his main concern when he came to see me for PTSD treatment.

Bret's transformation from junkyard dog to great white shark was important in his recovery. This signaled an acceptance of his actions as his own, not those of bad bad Leroy Brown. Bret also transformed himself in his dreams from young bull (running all the time) to old bull (riding the tidal wave, stopping the tidal wave, stopping to wait for the train), but he was still a "work in progress" in his personal life. As a police officer he had recovered from PTSD, and was able to return to work at full duty. Our last session was in December 2005, seven months after Bret's last reported dream (Dream 46).

TIPS FOR DREAM REVISION FROM CHAPTER 9

1. With an animal metaphor, as in Bret's Dream 5 (Junkyard Dog), it is best to stay within the metaphor. This was also the case with Kelly's Dream 9 (Chased by Snake) in Chapter 8. As therapy proceeded over time, Bret and I discussed the meaning of the junkyard dog metaphor, which was helpful in his recovery.
2. Over time, and with the appearance of a new metaphorical animal in Dream 33 (Great White Shark), Bret and I discussed the meaning of the new and old animal metaphors, which was helpful in the maturation of his personal identity.

TEN

Harassment: Dream Solutions for Waking Problems

Cindy was very distraught when she first came to see me. She tearfully apologized for being so upset; it was embarrassing to her. "I'm not usually like this," she told me. Between her tears, she was obsessed, hyperfocused on telling me the most minute details about recent events in her workplace. She was tremulous during the interview and admitted she had not wanted to take her anxiety medicine that morning, so she could drive safely from her home to my office.

Cindy was Caucasian, blond and attractive, 55 years old, divorced, with two grown children in their early thirties, and two grandchildren. Two months before coming to see me she had been taken off work by her family physician for acute stress.

She had been working as a therapist in the employee assistance program (EAP) of a government agency on contract with a private insurance company. Cindy and the other therapists worked for the insurance company. In the course of her work, Cindy became concerned about privacy violations involving the files of clients being seen in the EAP. She expressed her concern to several supervisors at the insurance company, but nothing was done, and the violations continued.

Cindy persisted in her complaints and then became concerned that she was being singled out by her supervisors as a troublemaker. She became upset about what she perceived as harassment and went to see her family physician, who took her off work and sent her to see me, because of my experience in the workers' compensation arena.

Cindy was born and raised in Southern California in an intact family. Her mother was loving and kind; her father was strict but intelligent and read to her as a child. An older sister died from a brain tumor. Both parents were now deceased as well. Cindy was dyslexic in school, but somehow managed to graduate from high school. Subsequently she completed both bachelor's and master's degrees in the field of psychology, and received an award for academic excellence from her university.

She had been married and divorced three times. Her two children were both from her first marriage, which lasted seven years from age 19 to 26. Her first husband, a physicist, considerably older than Cindy, became physically abusive when she insisted on going to college to earn a bachelor's degree. When Cindy showed her mother the bruises inflicted by her husband, Cindy's mother advised her to leave him, and have Cindy and the two children move in with her and Cindy's father. Cindy did this for a few years. Cindy's second marriage lasted eight years, beginning in her late twenties, and ended because of her husband's infidelity.

Between her second and third marriages Cindy got her license as a marriage, family, and child counselor (MFCC) and managed to build up a successful practice over a 10-year period in an upscale community north of San Diego. Cindy met her third husband on the Internet. He lived in the San Francisco Bay area and was from a very wealthy family. He encouraged Cindy to give up her practice, which had become somewhat stressful due to managed care, and to live with him near his family. She would not need to earn money as a therapist, but could teach psychology at a local college and run workshops at the Esalen Institute in nearby Big Sur on the coast. Cindy followed his suggestions, and they were married when Cindy was 49, but the marriage lasted only a year. "He was a hermit," she told me, "who needed to live alone." Cindy broke off the marriage and got a divorce settlement from the family, partly to compensate her for giving up her psychotherapy practice. Marrying her third husband was the first impulsive thing Cindy had done in her life, and it had been a big mistake.

A few years after divorcing her third husband she located a salaried job with her present employer, a managed care company. She had hoped to be able to match her private practice income without all the hassles of billing and collecting payments from clients and insurance companies.

I provided medication management and psychotherapy as treatment for Cindy. I made several important adjustments to Cindy's psychotropic medications during the course of her treatment. In the psychotherapy we functioned as allies; she was a skilled therapist in her own right, making important contributions to her successful recovery. I provided cognitive and supportive therapy in the form of discussion and analysis of Cindy's dreams. The inclusion of dreams in her treatment was Cindy's idea, as she shared a dream with me in her second session. I told her I was comfortable working with dreams in therapy, as I was already doing this with many PTSD patients in my practice. I did not mention dream revision therapy at that time, as I had not yet had enough exposure to Cindy's dreams.

During the course of her 18-month therapy with me, Cindy progressed from an initial state of extreme stress, with tearfulness, intrusive memories and flashbacks, scattered thoughts, hypervigilance and paranoia, to an eventual state of calm and firm determination, which allowed her to return to her work as a therapist. She did not return to her old job, due to her fractured relationship with her employer, but was able to find a suitable job with a different employer.

CINDY'S DREAMS

Cindy shared 40 dreams with me, which are listed and categorized in Table 10.1. Major themes and combinations of themes are indicated in the column on the far right. From these themes I identified the 3 most common ones: ANIMAL, WATER, and HOUSE. ANIMAL and WATER dreams overlapped considerably, as can be seen in Table 10.2, which lists 14 dreams dealing with one or both of these themes. Table 10.2 also includes several important events from Cindy's waking life for purposes of correlation with ANIMAL/WATER dream content. Cindy's 12 HOUSE dreams are listed in Table 10.3, along with the same life events from Table 5.2. Four HOUSE dreams that were also ANIMAL or WATER dreams are indicated by asterisks in Table 10.3. It is of interest that 3 of the 4 dreams marked by asterisks in Table 10.3 come late in the dream series, bringing together multiple themes as Cindy recovered and prepared to return to work.

As with earlier patients in this book (Andre in Chapter 5, Jack in Chapter 6, Bret in Chapter 9), Cindy's dreams have been divided up into groups based on events in her waking life. Dreams 1–14 in Table 10.1 constitute **Group 1 (Taken Off Work)**, from the beginning of our therapy sessions on 03/26/04 to my initiation of dream revision therapy on 7/22/04, about four months. Dreams 15–26 constitute **Group 2 (Dream Revision Therapy)**, from 07/22/04 to 01/13/05, when Cindy filed a civil lawsuit against her employer, about six months. Dreams 27–40 constitute **Group 3 (Civil Lawsuit Filed)**, from 01/13/05 to 07/21/05, when Cindy returned to work with a new employer, about six months. Individual dreams in Tables 10.2 and 10.3 are given numbers (1–3) to indicate the group they fall into.

Table 10.1 Dreams in a Therapist with Stress

#	Date	Dream Title	Lines	Theme
1	04/05/04	baby to care for	7	child
2	04/20/04	running the gauntlet	6	animal
3	04/29/04	orchard irrigation	13	animal/water
4	05/04/04	fired from teaching	2	job
5	05/11/04	2 a.m. party	16	house/(?co)
6	05/25/04	won my case	11	coworker
7		babysitting	10	child/therapy
8	06/08/04	riverboat	3	water
9		sick dog	10	house/animal
10		alcoholic neighbor	9	house
11	07/08/04	Russian conference	19	coworker/car
12		two therapists	12	therapy/child
13	07/22/04	d in my house	10	house/coworker
14		big bug	6	animal/(?co)
15	08/05/04	alligator bit my pants	10	animal/water
16	08/26/04	house tour	35	house
17		yoga	04	yoga(?co)
18	09/02/04	can't go to work	17	job/coworker
19	11/11/04	life book	3	therapy
20	11/18/04	surfing whales	13	animal/water
21		burn America	4	terrorist
22	11/29/04	letter from C	7	coworker
23	12/09/04	father at my door	8	house
24	12/23/04	alligator	2	animal/water
25	12/26/04	big snakes	8	men/anim/water
26	01/13/05	visit from F	11	house/coworker
27	02/03/05	river alligator	12	animal/water
28		son's snake	1	animal/house
29		adopted girl	1	child
30	02/14/05	acid rain with cat	29	ani/cowork/car
31		fifteen children	7	child/house
32	03/17/05	car thieves	6	cowork/hous/car

33	03/24/05	Robert De Niro	18	job/therap/men
34		gopher	11	job/coworker
35	04/08/05	metallic UFO	17	ca/an/hou/ch/wa
36	04/14/05	raft with cat	13	house/ani/water
37	05/10/05	locked in room	9	job
38	07/21/05	cheating husband	3	men/(?cowork)
39		cross-dressing husband	3	men/(?cowork)
40	09/29/05	Harrison Ford	5	car/men

Dreams Involving Animals or Water

As with Bret's dreams, we will examine Cindy's dreams one group at a time, beginning with the dreams in Table 10.2 and then moving on to the dreams in Table 10.3. There were five ANIMAL/WATER dreams in **Group 1 (Before Dream Revision Training)**.

Dream 2: 4/20/04 Running the Gauntlet

I'm in a big building, like a postal building. There are lots of boxes around, lots of metal racks. Yellow jackets (hornets) are on one side, with their bottoms sticking through. Brown rats are on the other side on wooden planks. I have to walk through without letting either side touch me. I get through. Then I wake up.

Dream 3: 4/29/04 Orchard Irrigation

(Scene 1) There are two high hedges. I'm walking through them toward a beautiful home. I'm in an orchard, which is very dry. The irrigation trenches are not dug deep enough. The water is not getting to the trees. I'm trying to water the trees, but this is not the way to do it. Things take time, my mother and you (Dr. Dow) are telling me, "Do it right. Let the water run through the trenches."

(Scene 2) A big tube of water is coming out the side, undermining the house. Elephants are wallowing in the mud, making the situation worse. I go down into the gully and try to push the elephants out. It's dangerous to be with them. I start with the small elephants, but there are big ones there too, dangerous ones. Then I wake up.

Table 10.2 Animal (A) and Water (W) Dreams (n=14)

#	Date	Dream Title/Event	Group	Months
	[01/15/04	**Taken Off Work]**		
	[03/26/04	**Initial Session]**		**4**
2	04/20/04	Running the Gauntlet	A	1
3	04/29/04	Orchard Irrigation	A,W	1
8	06/08/04	Riverboat	W	1
9		Sick Dog	A	1
14	07/22/04	Big Bug	A	1
	[07/22/04	**Dream Revision Therapy]**		**6**
15	08/05/04	Alligator Bit My Pants	A,W	2
20	11/18/04	Surfing Whales	A,W	2
24	12/23/04	Alligator	A,W	2
25	01/06/05	Big Snakes	A,W	2
	[01/13/05	**Civil Lawsuit Filed]**		**6**
27	02/03/05	River Alligator	A,W	3
28		Son's Snake	A	3
30	02/14/05	Acid Rain with Cat	A,W	3
35	04/08/05	Metallic UFO	A	3
36	04/14/05	Raft with Cat	A,W	3
	[07/21/05	**Return to Work]**		
	[08/09/05	**Civil Case Settled]**		

Dream 8: 06/08/04 Riverboat

We are going down a river in a boat that is out of control. The woman next to me is very afraid. I say, "Don't be afraid, everything will be OK."

Dream 9: 06/08/04 Sick Dog

I'm living in a nice house, very happy. I find a dog in my house. I pet it and give it a hug. What should I do with this dog? It's not mine. A neighbor woman comes over and says the dog is very sick and needs treatment. The scene switches, and we are riding in a car (the neighbor woman and me), taking the dog back to where it was getting treatment, but the facility is broken down. I take a good look at the dog. It is sick, all scabby under its stomach. The woman says I should turn it out and let it die. I say, "No, I don't think I can do that."

Dream 14: 07/22/04 Big Bug

My neighbor gives me this "Big Bug" for my birthday. It reminds me of my company. I decide I will send the Big Bug on to AB, my boss's boss at work. The message to him is, you kept the people who lied and were dishonest, which makes you a member of the bad bug gang. I wonder how I will explain to my neighbor that I gave away her gift.

At the time of Dream 2 (Running the Gauntlet) Cindy told me with tears in her eyes that her initial workers' compensation claim had been denied. She was feeling hopeless and seemed regressed and helpless, victimized, like an innocent little girl. Yet there is hope at the end of the dream: she manages to run the gauntlet and get through safely before waking up.

Dream 3 (Orchard Irrigation) is in some ways a continuation of Dream 2. The setting may be her grandparents' farm. Once again she is navigating between objects located at either side. Now she is getting help in the process, from both her mother and me. She is also confronting larger dangers, in the form of elephants. If the smaller dangers (insects, rodents) in Dream 2 represent her coworkers, the larger dangers (elephants) in Dream 3 may represent her supervisors and the large corporation they work for. Dream 3 is not as hopeful as Dream 2. Water appears in Dream 3, initially as part of the solution, but then it becomes part of the problem.

Dream 8 (Riverboat) continues the water theme in the form of a boat on a river. Part of Cindy is afraid; another part is more hopeful.

Dream 9 (Sick Dog) continues the animal theme in the form of a dog. The dog is sick and needs treatment. Cindy is the one who is getting treatment. The dream suggests she is very sick, even beyond treatment. Once again, part of Cindy is skeptical; another part is more hopeful. In this sense Dreams 8 and 9 are similar.

Dream 14 (Big Bug) makes a direct association between an animal ("big bug") and Cindy's employer. This supports our earlier suggestion that (big) elephants in Dream 3 referred to her employer.

Following Dreams 13 and 14, which Cindy shared with me on the same day, I discussed with Cindy the technique of dream revision, to assist her with revising Dream 13 (see below, with the HOUSE dreams).

There were four ANIMAL/WATER dreams in **Group 2 (After Dream Revision Training)**.

Dream 15: 08/05/04 Alligator Bit My Pants

I am at a lawn party in Florida with a group of people. I'm arguing with them, in a friendly, not hostile, way. One group is in front of me, and another group is on the sidelines. I'm getting the better of the argument. The people on the side say, "Well, look what just happened to you." I turn around, and see that a big alligator has just bit my pants. It is like a cartoon. How am I going to get this alligator off my butt? If I turn around, it will really bite me. I'm not too afraid, just trying to figure out how to get this alligator to let go of me.

Dream 20: 11/18/04 Surfing Whales

I'm out walking on the beach. It's a beautiful beach. I would like to live here. I see dolphins. Then I see all these seals jump into the air, hundreds of them. At first I am afraid that someone has bombed them, but there is no bomb; they are just really happy. It is an amazing beach, with just a few people on it, neither crowded nor deserted. I see a whale right up close to the shore. Somehow the water is deep enough for it to swim without getting beached. Then another whale goes by; people in wetsuits are standing on it. Then a third whale goes by, this time with people in regular clothes standing on it, standing on the fin, looking at me and waving. It's the most amazing place. I could ride one of those waves. If they could do it, I could do it too.

Dream 24: 12/23/04 Alligator

An alligator is coming out of the water to pull me under. I had to run up the hill to get away from it.

Dream 25: 01/06/05 Big Snakes

I'm with a man, an Esalen-type guru man. I feel untrusting of him. He has a group of followers. He wants me to be his first follower. He doesn't seem that interested in me. Everyone walks down to this lake, a swampy lake, a big lake. I get real scared. I say everyone should run up the hill. Big snakes come out of the lake, their heads bigger than their tails. It is a forest of snakes, with big teeth. Everyone runs up the hill to get away from them.

Dream 15 (Alligator Bit My Pants) is the first of several alligator dreams in the series. After Dream 3 (Orchard Irrigation) and Dream 14 (Big Bug), it may not be far-fetched to associate the alligator of Dream 15 with Cindy's employer. The animals in Dreams 3 and 14 seemed dangerous. The alligator in Dream 15 actually bites Cindy's pants.

Given our earlier dream revision session following Dream 13 (see below and Tables 10.2 and 10.3), it was fascinating to me that Cindy was already thinking about how to extricate herself from the alligator. She was actually attempting to do dream revision within the dream, though she may have rehearsed this in advance of falling asleep. My goal in teaching dream revision to Cindy was not specifically to make her a lucid dreamer,[1] but this seemed on the verge of happening in Dream 15. She already knew from her own considerable insight and from our earlier discussions that hostile animals in her dreams probably represented her employer. She knew from our discussion after Dream 13 that she had the power to do something about this. In Dream 15 she is trying to take action. She knows she is in a cartoon. Does she also know she is the cartoonist? She only needs to draw the next picture, showing how she manages to get the alligator to stop biting her pants and leave her alone.

Dream 15 is a key dream in the series, the beginning of the end of Cindy's oppression by hostile animals. The process will take some time, however. She still has a number of similar dreams ahead of her. She understands that dream revision is possible, but needs to figure out how to accomplish it. She is working toward becoming a resourceful survivor rather than a helpless victim.

Perhaps our discussion after Dream 15 was helpful, since Dream 20 (Surfing Whales), the next ANIMAL/WATER dream in the series, is considerably more upbeat than Dream 15. Dream 20, like Dream 9 (Sick Dog), seems to represent Cindy in animal form, namely, as a group of dolphins. The dreamer specifically identifies herself with the dolphins: "I could ride one of those waves." This is a healing dream. Cindy has definitely made progress from the sick dog of Dream 9.

Dreams 24, 25, 27, 28, and 35 all involve alligators or snakes. Dreams 24 (Alligator) and 27 (River Alligator) are essentially recurrences of Dream 15, in slightly modified form. Dreams 25, 28, and 35 are about snakes. Dream 25 (Big Snakes) recurred three times, shortly after the tsunami in the Indian Ocean on 12/26/04, which killed 230,000 people in south Asia. Cindy incorporates the tsunami into her dream series in the form of a forest of big snakes which arise out of a lake.

There were five ANIMAL/WATER dreams in **Group 3 (After Civil Lawsuit Filing)**.

Dream 27: 02/03/05 River Alligator

I'm on a vacation trip on a river with other people on a big boat. The river goes out to the ocean in a delta area. There is vegetation on the banks. There are large floating wooden steps that we are supposed to get up on, sit on the step part, and float down the river. I'm concerned. I ask, "There are no alligators in this river, are there?" A guy says, "No, they are further down." Five people get on the steps with me, including two young men. The guide is a young guy. I see that we are going to float down into this marshy area. The guy says to look through that fence. A huge alligator pops out. I and some other people run away from the river, across a low cut hay field, up a hill.

Dream 28: 02/03/05 Son's Snake

I let my son have a snake. We are looking for it in the house.

Dream 30: 02/14/05 Acid Rain with Cat

I have my cat with me, driving in the car (this is not normal). My cat is in the backseat, not in a cat box (also not normal). We are going to the veterinarian. I get out of the car, my cat on my shoulder. It is raining bubbles. I say to my cat, "This is amazing." The bubbles begin moving horizontally, coming toward us, like a squall. One of them hits me. It feels like acid. "Oh my God," I say, "these are dangerous." People will get hurt by these bubbles. Help will be available for people, but not for cats. I put my cat under my coat to protect it. I am upset and irritated.

I'm now trying to get home. By mistake I drive onto the wrong ramp of the freeway, but then it merges and is OK. Traffic is heavy. I see a motorcycle cop behind me with flashing lights but no siren. I can't find a place to stop the car. Now it's just raining. I can't get off this freeway. Can't the cop see this? Oh, fuck! There is a sandy turnoff, but it slopes down at the edge. There are old yellow weeds. I pull off onto the sandy turnoff, and the cop pulls off behind me. I kind of ski my car to a stop, whipping the rear end around. The rear end starts to go off the embankment. I pick up the car and put it back on level ground. My cat has gotten out of the car and has run away. The cop says, "I have to arrest you; you didn't pull over soon enough." The cop is a woman with blond hair in a ponytail (Cindy's supervisor, C, had blond hair, but not in a ponytail; Cindy also has blond hair.). I am fighting back, not agreeing that I have done anything wrong. I decide to go find my cat. I wake up, and my cat is sitting on my shoulder.

Dream 35: 04/08/05 Metallic UFO

I'm in a cab, going to Mexico (Tijuana) to go shopping. I decide it's too expensive to take the cab all the way to Mexico. I'm talking to the cab driver. He is very nice and has a family. We see a black meadow in the sky. Is it a government experimental vehicle? It moves in front of the cab and has a silver, metallic, corrugated appearance. It has arms that come out, like snakes. It is definitely not a government experimental vehicle. I say to the cab driver, "I'm going home." He drives me home, and I go into my apartment. The building is starting to shake. Two people are in my apartment with a baby. I tell them to get away from the windows. They say there is a big black thing coming over. My cat looks out the window as the thing passes over and starts having a seizure, which continues as long as he looks at the thing. I put the cat in a closet and the seizure stops. I'm in a dark space with no windows. There is a metallic clicking noise. I know it's from the thing in the sky.

Dream 36: 04/14/05 Raft with Cat

I'm lying in bed; my cat is in bed with me. I roll over, and there is a giant cat in bed with me (with a zipper costume on). It's a cat that goes after rats (a ratter). I unzip it, and there is a little cat inside, a little smaller than my cat. I know this cat is special, like a magic cat. I want to keep it, even though it's not the kind of cat you can keep. It starts to run away. My cat and I run after it. We all jump onto these palm leaves that are floating in this clear ocean (the South Seas). I'm just lying there floating along, floating out with the tide. It feels so good, with the sun on my face. I want to just keep floating, but I realize we have to get off the raft to keep from floating out to sea. We get off the raft. The magic cat runs away.

Dream 27 (River Alligator) is the last of three alligator dreams in the series, and this alligator is "huge," perhaps bigger than the earlier ones in Dreams 15 and 24. The other two alligator dreams preceded the tsunami of 12/26/04 in the Indian Ocean. Dream 27 came after the tsunami, which could explain the increase in size of the alligator. Nevertheless, Cindy does not seem particularly afraid of the alligator in Dream 27. She simply runs away from it up a hill, just as she did in Dream 27. The alligator is in no danger of biting her pants.

Dream 28 (Son's Snake) is about looking for her son's snake in the house. Though it seems innocent enough, the notion of a snake in (or near) her house is not a pleasant one for Cindy, as we also see in Dream 35, and will discuss further in the next dream sub-series, involving HOUSE dreams.

Dreams 30 (Acid Rain with Cat) and 36 (Raft with Cat) involve Cindy and her beloved cat, who provides companionship and may act as a protector. Dream 30 is a nightmare about acid rain and a somewhat hostile female police officer, reminiscent of Cindy's supervisor. Cindy's cat is present in the dream and is sitting on Cindy's shoulder when she wakes up.

Dream 35 (Metallic UFO) includes an enormous and ominous space craft which hovers over her taxicab and later her home and has "arms that come out, like snakes." This object would seem to represent Cindy's employer, whose corporate name is suggestive of a space vehicle.

Dream 36 (Raft with Cat) is perhaps the most upbeat, happy dream in the entire series of 40 dreams, with Cindy and her cat lying on palm leaves and floating on the ocean in the South Seas. Coming so late in the series, Dream 36 seems to be a recovery dream. Just three months after this dream she was back at work. The two themes of ANIMALS and WATER are nicely synthesized in Dream 36.

In a sense, the ANIMAL dreams play out a battle between animals representing Cindy's employer and hostile coworkers (yellow jackets, rats, elephants, big bugs, alligators, and snakes) and animals representing Cindy (dog, dolphins, cat), with WATER being a typical (though not essential) setting. Cindy emerges victorious in Dream 36, along with her cat. There is a childlike quality to this dream series, with Cindy's cat as protector, like a teddy bear or other stuffed animal.

Another patient of mine utilized a whole series of stuffed animals (snail, lion, mouse, buffalo) in her healing dreams, eventually settling on the buffalo, perhaps because it was large and furry like a lion, but not so dangerous.

It seems likely in Cindy's case that dream revision sessions following Dreams 13 and 15 played an important role in the evolution of her ANIMAL/WATER dreams. There is a clear progression in these dreams from danger and sickness to hope and healing.

Dreams Involving Cindy's House

We now turn our attention to the HOUSE dreams of Table 10.3. There are four HOUSE dreams in **Group 1 (Before Dream Revision Training)**, one of which, Dream 9 (Sick Dog) was also an ANIMAL dream and has already been discussed.

Table 10.3 House Dreams (n=12)

#	Date	Dream Title/Event	Group	Months
	[01/15/04	**Taken Off Work]**		
	[03/26/04	**Initial Session]**		**4**
5	05/11/04	Two AM Party	1	
9	06/08/04	*Sick Dog	1	
10		Alcoholic Neighbor	1	
13	07/22/04	D in My House	1	
	[07/22/04	**Dream Revision Therapy]**		**6**
16	08/26/04	House Tour	2	
23	12/09/04	Father at My Door	2	
	[01/13/05	**Civil Lawsuit Filed]**		**6**
26	01/13/05	Visit from F	3	
28	02/03/05	*Son's Snake	3	
31		Fifteen Children	3	
32	03/17/05	Car Thieves	3	
35	04/08/05	*Metallic UFO	3	
36	04/14/05	*Raft with Cat	3	
	[07/21/05	**Return to Work]**		
	[08/09/05	**Civil Case Settled]**		

* also ANIMAL and/or WATER dreams

Dream 5: 5/11/04 2 a.m. Party

It's 2 a.m. I'm hearing all this partying noise outside. I get up to find out what it is. Outside I see garbage cans overflowing with trash, including beer bottles. Next to the garbage cans is a truck with young people partying in it. Also in the truck is an adult woman about my age. I go around looking for my long pants to put on. The lights are not working in my house. One light is working, but it's in the wrong part of the house. I unscrew it and try to take it to the other part of the house and screw it in, but in the darkness I can't find the fixture to screw it into. I find my long pants. I tell people they can't party there. They say they won't leave. I say I will wake up the landlord. They say they are friends of the landlord. I say I will call the police. They say that will get me in trouble with the landlord. Feeling frustrated, I wake up.

Dream 10: 06/08/04 Alcoholic Neighbor

A neighbor woman across the patio has been fighting with my neighbors, though I get along with her. She sent a note to a neighbor man saying he was gay because he wouldn't go out with her. She drinks a lot. She wanders into my apartment, saying it is hers. She has been drinking. The neighbors are trying to get her out of the apartment. I say to her, just do what you want. She then realizes that it isn't her house. Her family helps get her back across the patio to her house.

Dream 13: 07/22/04 D in My House

I'm living in a nice house. My coworker, D is renting a room in my house. I know everything she has done at work. She is getting into my stuff, using my towels and other things. She looks younger; I look older (but not wiser). I confront her: "You have to move out of my house." She says, "I don't know what you're talking about." How much notice do I have to give her? Maybe I will give her seven days' notice. I tell her off. She doesn't seem to care. She says, "This isn't a big deal, because I'm going to work." I get really angry and wake up.

Dream 5 (2 a.m. Party) takes place in Cindy's house. In relation to Cindy's waking life, the party would appear to represent her workplace, where patients' charts had been left out in the waiting room area, compromising their confidentiality. The dreamer's threats to wake up the landlord or call the police correspond to Cindy's efforts to report the workplace confidentiality violations to her supervisors at the insurance company. In this sense, the party people could represent Cindy's coworkers in the employee assistance program (EAP), with the dreamer (Cindy) representing herself, the whistle-blower.

Cindy told me she had this dream after trying again and again to reach a particular attorney to take her workers' compensation case. Eventually, she managed to get another more feisty attorney whom she preferred. The dream itself is frustrating, but she is not a victim here. She is definitely taking action, though it isn't yet clear what that action will be: waking up the landlord or calling the police. The important thing about Dream 5 is not what she actually does, but that she asserts herself regarding the noisy 2 a.m. partying by her neighbors. She is not going to put up with it, just as she is not going to put up with the confidentiality violations that are occurring at her workplace in waking life. This is an important dream in the series, presenting itself to Cindy in symbolic form.

Dream 10 (Alcoholic Neighbor) is about a female neighbor who gets drunk and wanders into Cindy's apartment, claiming it as her own. Like Dream 5, this is probably about Cindy's coworkers, with the alcoholic neighbor of Dream 10 corresponding to the party people of Dream 5. The home invasion has become more intrusive in Dream 10; in Dream 5 the neighbors did not actually enter Cindy's house. Fortunately, the home invader in Dream 10 leaves without Cindy having to take any action.

In Dream 13 (D in My House), for the first time in the series, we see actual invasion of Cindy's house by her coworker, D. Furthermore, the coworker didn't just wander in (and out), as in Dream 10, but is actually staying in Cindy's house and seems unwilling to leave, despite Cindy's efforts. A threshold has clearly been reached with Dream 13, as Cindy realizes in her dream. She wakes up angry from this dream. On the day that Cindy shared this dream with me she told me she was having problems with acid reflux. Her anger was beginning to irritate her stomach and esophagus. Something had to be done.

After hearing Dream 13 from Cindy, I suggested she try dream revision therapy on it, since home invasion by coworkers was turning into a recurrent theme. Cindy's initial impulse in revising the dream was to hit her coworker, but I suggested a more refined solution: getting the coworker arrested and sent to jail. Cindy liked this idea, and agreed to work on it. It was gratifying to her to be able to take action in her dream and not simply endure the abuse by her coworker(s).

There are two HOUSE dreams in **Group 2 (After Dream Revision Training)**.

Dream 16: 08/26/04 House Tour

(Scene 1) I'm in a house. My daughter lives there too, as well as other college students. It's a student place. I'm dressed in things I wear at home, comfortable clothes. I just washed my hair, haven't yet had time to curl it. The kids (students) are out of the house. A black woman comes to the door, nicely dressed in a suit, about 40 years old. She says that she has come to see the house where Stephanie (my daughter) lives. I say, "We weren't expecting you." She insists that she needs to see the house.

(Scene 2) I start to show her around. I show her a room with a king-sized bed. Three kids sleep in it. It has a beautiful view, across the housetops to the ocean beyond. I feel nervous, uncomfortable with her. I make the light

comment that if she were looking for a house, she could see from this window which ones were good. I do this to distract her, but she indicates she wants to see other rooms. I show her a room with a row of beds, including my bed (not made). I start making my bed. She says she wants to see the bathroom. Then she says, "You're going with me now to meet the other families whose children are going into this college program." (my daughter wants to get into a nursing program).

(Scene 3) She says, "We have to go right now." I take off my flip-flops. We go. Everyone looks impeccable. I'm wearing my old shorts with holes and an old comfortable short-sleeved top. At the entrance to the building, people are walking in. It looks like a library building, with columns, a peaked roof, an elegant entrance. I stand out on the steps. I say, "I can't go in there dressed like this." She says, "You have to." I say, "You have to judge my daughter on her own merits. Don't make your decision based on me. It would be as if someone based your ability to go to school on whether you were black or white." She calls me a racist.

(Scene 4) A young white man, in his thirties, tall, well dressed in a suit and tie, tells me I have to go. I say no. I go to an In and Out burger and order a vegetarian (cheese) sandwich. I feel stupid.

Dream 23: 12/09/04 Father at My Door

I have just gotten out of the shower and put my regular clothes on. I am dressed in shorts; my hair is all sticking out. A man is outside my door, age 45 or so, wearing red shorts, in good health. I recognize him as my father at that age. He has short hair, like in the fifties. He is happy to see me, and I am happy to see him. He says, "Everyone should have a Christmas gift. I just wanted you to know that your family loves you." I wake up feeling great.

Dream 16 (House Tour) is the longest dream in the entire series. A black woman has come to look at Cindy's house. The woman in a sense takes over the house and Cindy as well, but we never find out who she is. The woman takes Cindy, dressed in her casual clothes, to a building with columns, a peaked roof, and an elegant entrance, which could represent the courthouse where Cindy's legal cases will be decided (three months later for the first case, 12 months later for the second case). The black woman is nicely dressed in a suit and seems hostile to Cindy; perhaps she is the attorney for Cindy's employer, who will be opposing Cindy in court in the near future. Dream 16 was clearly threatening to Cindy, though neither she nor I knew exactly what to make of it at the time she told it to me.

Between Dream 16 and Dream 23 Cindy achieved several financial victories in her waking life. On 7/29/04 she told me she was bothered by an incident in which her car mechanic had overcharged her for an oil change. Four months later, on 11/23/04, she went back to the oil change facility and complained to them about her experience on 7/29/04. They gave her back her money. This was gratifying to Cindy, not so much for the money, but as a metaphor for her work situation. She was learning to be assertive and having some success with it. Her workers' compensation case settled for cash on 11/18/04. On that same date she had reported to me an upbeat ANIMAL/WATER dream, Dream 20 (Surfing Whales). Both her waking life and her dream life were showing signs of improvement.

Dream 23 (Father at My Door) is a HOUSE dream involving a visit from Cindy's father. This dream, like Dream 20 of the ANIMAL/WATER series, is upbeat and hopeful. The support of her family, symbolized by her father, means a lot to her. She seems to have turned the corner, though she still has some hazards to navigate.

There are six HOUSE dreams in **Group 3 (After Civil Lawsuit Filing)**, three of which, Dreams 28 (Son's Snake), 35 (Metallic UFO), and 36 (Raft with Cat), were also ANIMAL/WATER dreams and have been discussed.

Dream 26: 01/13/05 Visit from R

R, a former colleague who works in San Francisco, shows up in my apartment with her bags. How wonderful for her to come and see me. We can't talk about my employer, so we talk about the weather. She stays on my sofa. This street person is hanging around. R and I go for a walk to the bay. The street person comes into my house and makes a bed in it. I throw his bedding out the door. I don't want to get physical with him. He comes after me with a knife. R stabs him with a small knife, causing just a small wound. Then he goes after her. I call someone to come and help me. I want everyone to come. They just mill around. Then I wake up.

Dream 31: 02/14/05 Fifteen Children

I have this huge family of children, at least 15, all adopted, with ages ranging from 9 to 12. I'm responsible for them. They are good children, running around, not doing anything bad. I have to get organized to take care of them all. I get them organized to do different chores. I apologize to them, saying there is not enough time to love you all. I wake up feeling good.

Dream 32: 03/17/05 Car Thieves

My car is in my driveway. It's a nice car. Two women are in the car, trying to steal it. I go up to the window, which is rolled down. I tell them to get out of my car. It looks like my coworkers, D and C. They start backing the car out of my driveway. I reach in the window, open the door, and pull out the driver (I'm not sure whether it's D or C).

Dream 26 (Visit from R) involves a visit from Cindy's San Francisco friend and former colleague, R. This is a supportive dream, like Dream 23, except for the street person, another intruder, perhaps representing Cindy's coworkers. After a scuffle of sorts, R ends up stabbing the intruder and causing a small wound. The fact that Cindy has a friend in her house to protect her from invaders is significant and hopeful. In a sense, Cindy has two coworkers in her house, one friendly, the other unfriendly. Shortly after this dream, Cindy began looking at job openings.

Dream 28 (Son's Snake) is about invasion of her HOUSE by a snake, a hostile animal representing Cindy's employers and coworkers, as described earlier.

Dream 31 (Fifteen Children) is indirectly about Cindy's HOUSE, as a place where she takes care of 15 or more adopted children. No invaders are present. The dream is upbeat and positive.

Dream 32 (Car Thieves) is a car invasion dream by coworkers. This is a HOUSE dream, since the car is parked in the driveway of her house. The coworkers are trying to steal her car. She reaches into the window and stops them. No need for dream revision therapy here. Cindy has thwarted the attempted car theft. In this sense, Dream 32 is upbeat. Cindy seems like a survivor here rather than a victim. She has learned to be oneirically (in her dreams) assertive toward her coworkers.

Dream 35 (Metallic UFO), previously discussed as an ANIMAL/WATER dream, involves the invasion of Cindy's HOUSE from the sky in the form of a spaceship with metallic arms that makes the whole building shake and causes Cindy's cat to have a seizure. Fortunately, Dream 35 was followed only one week later by Dream 36.

The last HOUSE dream of the series, Dream 36 (Raft with Cat), also included in Table 5.2 as an ANIMAL/WATER dream, begins with Cindy and her beloved cat alone in her house. Her cat has rid the house of rats, and the home invasion is over. In Dream 36 Cindy feels good about herself and her new life.

Cindy had the interview for her new job in April 2005. In May 2005 she told me she had gotten the job and would be starting soon. Some problems developed in the resolution of her civil case against her employer, and we focused our attention in therapy on this issue. Cindy's coworkers were reluctant to exonerate Cindy from future lawsuits they might choose to bring against her.

In July 2005 Cindy told me she had begun seeing clients and getting paid for it. In August 2005 she said her case was settling out of court, and she was working as a therapist and enjoying it. In our last session on 9/29/05 she indicated she had stopped all psychotropic medications and did not need further sessions with me. She felt like a survivor. She was amazed at how much she had managed to get through.

TRAUMA DREAMS VS. STRESS DREAMS

It is useful to compare the dreams of Bret from Chapter 9 and Cindy from the present chapter, since Bret suffered from PTSD, while Cindy's diagnosis was work-related stress, currently coded as "adjustment disorder." Both patients were seen from about the time they were taken off work to the point of full recovery and return to work. Cindy was back to work in 18 months; Bret was back to work in 31 months. The total number of dreams was roughly the same for the two patients: 46 for Bret, 40 for Cindy.

Bret and Cindy were both adept at interpreting their dreams, Cindy from the beginning, Bret with some coaching. I taught dream revision therapy to each of them about one third of the way into their respective dream series, after Dream 13 (D in My House) for Cindy, after Dream 17 (Undercover Cop) for Bret. Each indicated they subsequently made an effort to apply dream revision techniques to deal with nightmares.

Bret was initially tormented by recurrent dreams of BEING CHASED. Prior to initiation of dream revision therapy, his BEING CHASED dreams were repetitive, like a broken record. After initiation of dream revision therapy, his BEING CHASED dreams changed more quickly, though they were still present (in modified form) almost a year after his return to full duty.

With Cindy it was more difficult to see recurrent patterns in her dreams. One pattern involved ANIMALS that were either threatening or nonthreatening (protective). Eventually, the protective animals won out. Another pattern involved coworkers invading her HOUSE. Eventually the coworkers were driven out. Reviewing Cindy's dreams, we never get the sense of a broken record, as with Bret's dreams. Each of Cindy's dreams is unique, though trends and patterns can be identified. Cindy did not get stuck in her dreams to the degree that Bret did.

Bret and Cindy both showed substantial benefit from a relatively small amount of dream revision training. Their recovery process is revealed in their dreams, once the dreams are categorized by theme. Restricting dream analysis to a few themes at a time (BEING CHASED for Bret; ANIMALS, WATER, HOUSE for Cindy) permits sequential patterns to be identified. Such patterns were not readily detectable in either dream series in the absence of categorization by theme.

TIPS FOR DREAM REVISION FROM CHAPTER 10

1. Dream revision principles in this chapter may not be directly applicable to PTSD treatment, as Cindy was not suffering from PTSD. Her DSM-IV TR psychiatric diagnosis was "adjustment disorder with mixed anxiety and depressed mood."
2. Furthermore, Cindy was herself a therapist and quite aware of metaphorical meanings of dreams. I taught her the principles of dream revision following Dreams 13 (D in My House) and 15 (Alligator Bit My Pants). Cindy used her knowledge to protect herself (oneirically, in her dreams) from hostile animals by surrounding herself with friendly animals. After being threatened by an alligator in Dream 15, she used aquatic mammals (dolphins, seals, whales) to change her mood in Dream 20 (Surfing Whales). After being threatened by snakes in Dream 35 (Metallic UFO), she used her cat as a magical protector in Dream 36 (Raft with Cat).
3. Cindy's recognition that she had the ability to change her dreams helped her gain the courage in waking life to file and win two lawsuits against her employer, the first for workers compensation benefits, the second for personal injury benefits.

ELEVEN

Brain Mechanisms of PTSD and Recovery

The current definition of posttraumatic stress disorder (PTSD) in the official Diagnostic and Statistical Manual of Mental Disorders, Fourth Edition (DSM-IV TR) involves "intense fear, helplessness, or horror" through the witnessing or experiencing of a life-threatening event.[1] Helplessness is a central feature of the entire PTSD symptom complex.

The American psychologist Martin Seligman identified "learned helplessness" as an important syndrome in humans and animals.[2] PTSD is thought to be a condition associated with learned helplessness.[3] The key to recovering from PTSD is to overcome the feeling of helplessness.

Recent brain imaging studies of people suffering from PTSD have shown localized changes in brain regions involved in emotion, namely, the amygdala and the medial prefrontal cortex.[4] Normally, the amygdala, a brain nucleus located beneath the temporal lobe of the cerebral cortex, is regulated by the medial prefrontal cortex. In patients with PTSD the amygdala is overactive, and the medial prefrontal cortex is underactive.

The medial prefrontal cortex is an important center for "volition" or "will," the mental ability to make decisions and initiate actions.[5] To initiate an action we must decide which of several possible actions to initiate. Our emotions provide the information we need. It is not simply by chance that a major brain center for emotion is also associated with volition.

The goal in treating PTSD is to overcome helplessness. The amygdala has taken over. The volitional center in the cerebral cortex must regain control. Using now outmoded but prescient Freudian terms from the early 20th century, the "Id" needs to be brought under the control of the "Superego."[6]

Revising a dream is a convenient way to overcome helplessness. It is convenient because we think of dreams as stories. We can change a story more easily than we can change a terrible life event. Unfortunately, nightmares can come perilously close to depicting actual life events. However, nightmares are still stories, being replayed over and over in our minds night after night, sometimes all night long, at 90-minute intervals.

Fortunately, nightmares usually deviate from actual life events, sometimes in subtle ways. This allows us to get a handle on them. If the nightmare already deviates even slightly from the traumatic life event, then why can't we just tweak it a bit so it deviates more? Anything we can do to overcome the feeling of helplessness is a step on the road to recovery.

Once we get a handle on the nightmare, there is no limit to the changes we can make. We can bring in anything we need from the outside world. What kind of help would we prefer? It is as if we have a Genie (like Aladdin) or a Fairy Godmother (like Cinderella). We have only to wish for something and we can get it.

Fairy tales are an excellent example of frightening situations being magically and miraculously given happy endings. The psychiatrist Bruno Bettelheim describes this function of fairy tales in his helpful book, *The Uses of Enchantment: The Meaning and Importance of Fairy Tales*.

When changing nightmares into dreams, it is essential to stay as focused as possible. Just work on one nightmare at a time, usually the worst one, the one causing the most sleep disturbance. Try to make as few changes as possible, since it will be easier to rehearse and memorize them. The changes should be believable. This will make it easier for you to accept them as possibly having occurred.

One exception to the believable change rule, especially with traumas from the distant past, is to bring something into the dream from your waking present. For example, a cell phone might be helpful in a nightmare from, say 20 or 30 years ago, when there were no cell phones. A modern self-defense weapon such as a Taser might be helpful in such dreams as well. Before choosing to use a Taser in your dream, you might want to learn more about how Tasers work. You need to research your story as carefully as possible to make it plausible, even as science fiction. If you were abused as a child, it can be helpful to bring yourself as an adult (possibly with a current trusted companion or a police officer) back into the nightmare abuse scene of your childhood. As a reviser of dreams, you are becoming a writer, making up a fictional fantasy story about yourself.

Many people with PTSD find it hard to confront their nightmares when fully awake. They try to forget about their nightmares just as they try to forget about their trauma. Some trauma survivors may manage to do this and recover on their own. However, once nightmares become established, they tend to get worse and worse, like a bad infection, until one makes the decision to take action and seek help.

Just as one goes to a doctor for help with a bad infection, one may go to a doctor for help with a recurrent nightmare, but the usual medical treatments for anxiety, stress, and sleep disturbance are not particularly helpful for PTSD. At the time of this writing the two most useful medications for treating posttraumatic nightmares, and PTSD in general, are trazodone for help in falling asleep and prazosin for help in staying asleep.[7] Trazodone (Desyrel) is an older antidepressant that is not addicting but quite sedating; in low doses it becomes a good sleeping pill. Prazosin (Minipress) is an older medication for high blood pressure; it has been shown to block nightmares, perhaps by reducing input to the amygdala.[8] To use prazosin safely one needs to monitor blood pressure regularly. Both trazodone and prazosin require prescriptions, though not necessarily from a psychiatrist. Both are available in generic form for only a few pennies per pill.

It is important to be patient when trying to change a nightmare, especially one that has been going on for some time. A nightmare is a kind of "habit" the brain has gotten into. One can't expect to change it all at once, though occasionally this does happen. More commonly, one sees gradual changes over time (weeks to months). The key thing is for the nightmare to deviate more and more from the actual traumatic events. Any intrusion into the nightmare from one's other memory stores (past or recent) is welcome. Once the nightmare begins to change in major ways, it will likely break up and go away.

Sometimes a proposed dream change doesn't work at all. Don't give up. Just go back to the drawing board and try a different change. Often one gains insights into the nightmare as one tries to change it. One sees a possible change point that one hadn't noticed before. Sometimes the dream changes just a little, but continues to be a problem. In such cases a different change is worth trying, as it may be more potent, that is, more effective in altering the dream than one's first attempt was.

Some people, especially combat veterans but also civilians, suffer from guilt over trauma resulting from their own actions or lack of action. Several of my patients have raised concerns about the morality of changing a dream that accurately depicts something they did that was wrong. The issue of atonement comes up in such cases. Can dream revision function as forgiveness of one's sins? Is it morally wrong to forgive one's own sins?

Careful review of the traumatic situation, either by oneself or with a therapist (or religious counselor), may suggest that the guilt is unwarranted. For a veteran, perhaps the combat situation called for a certain action. For a civilian, perhaps they were too young and innocent at the time of the trauma to be fully responsible for the events that took place.

In some situations the guilt may be warranted. If one feels truly guilty, it may be necessary to come up with a "repayment" plan, for example, a volunteer service activity in the community, directed toward a group one has wronged, or perhaps some other form of payback. Here the goal is to transform negative karma into positive karma. The purpose of dream revision is not to help perpetrators escape punishment for crimes, but to help them reform and cease committing acts that cause them (and others) to have nightmares.

It may be helpful to use prazosin along with dream revision to reduce the intensity of the nightmare, and thereby make it easier to work with. One might be tempted to let prazosin do all the work; however, the problem with using prazosin alone is that the nightmare can return whenever one misses a few doses of the medicine. Changing the dream through dream revision is a more permanent solution to the problem.

Ultimately, what is called for in recovery from PTSD is "will" or "volition." One needs to become a survivor rather than a victim. One needs to become resilient. One needs to fight off the nightmare the way we talk about "fighting" off cancer. Cancer was once thought to be incurable. Many cancers are now curable with appropriate therapy. PTSD was also once thought to be incurable. The message of this book is that PTSD is curable. The cure may take time, but as the stories in this book illustrate, a complete cure is possible, with dream revision as an ongoing technique to fight off any new nightmares that may arise.

Recent research studies[9] have increased our understanding of "conditioned fear," which seems relevant to PTSD. Following a trauma, any sensory reminder of the trauma (a sight, sound, touch, taste, or smell) is capable of re-creating the entire trauma experience in the form of a flashback. The flashback then becomes a new trauma, which is consolidated into long-term memory, most likely during sleep. Emotional memories, involving both the amygdala (emotion center of the brain) and the hippocampus (memory center of the brain), are consolidated during rapid eye movement (REM) sleep, when our most vivid dreaming occurs.[10] The consolidation of a flashback, reaching consciousness as a nightmare (replaying the original trauma), is effectively a reconsolidation.

It is now becoming apparent that memory reconsolidation presents an opportunity to revise the original memory: to soften it, make it less frightening, and more bearable. In untreated PTSD, there is no softening. The trauma memory tends to get stronger rather than weaker, presumably by means of repeated flashbacks and nightmares. Exposure therapy for PTSD (prolonged exposure or PE, eye movement desensitization and reprocessing or EMDR) runs the risk of strengthening the trauma memory, especially in the therapist is inexperienced.

Dream revision therapy differs from exposure therapy in that its goal is not just to recall the trauma, but to change it, weaken it, and eventually make it go away. If PTSD is a form of conditioned fear, dream revision therapy for PTSD is a powerful method to enhance extinction.

Notes

CHAPTER 1: RESCRIPT YOUR DREAMS AND RECOVER FROM PTSD

1. Five such cases are illustrated in this book, one in the present chapter (Tom), and four others in Chapters 3–6 (Carlos, Andre, Gary, and Jack).
2. Krakow et al. 2001; Forbes et al. 2003; Moore and Krakow 2007.
3. American Psychiatric Association (APA) DSM-IV, TR 2000.
4. Dow et al. 1996.
5. Yoshioka et al. 1996; Dow 2002.
6. Davidson and Foa 1993, pp. ix–xiii.
7. Shay 1994, 2002.
8. Davidson and Foa 1993, pp. xii.
9. APA DSM-IV, TR 2000.
10. Ross et al. 1989; Raskind et al. 2003, 2013; Taylor et al. 2008; Bajor et al. 2011.
11. Freud 1900, pp. 155–166.
12. Years later, Freud modified his dream theory to include anxiety dreams and punishment dreams as well as wishful dreams (Freud 1933, pp. 8–37).
13. Foa and Meadows 1997; Foa and Rothbaum 1998; Hembree and Foa 2003.
14. Shapiro 2001, 2002, 2013; Shapiro and Maxfield 2002.

CHAPTER 2: DREAM TEAM

1. Dow et al. 1996.
2. Ross et al. 1989.
3. Taylor et al. 1997.
4. Krakow et al. 2001.

CHAPTER 6: RETRAUMATIZATION AND RECOVERY

1. Now Los Angeles County Hospital, University of Southern California (USC) Medical Center.
2. Anch et al. 1988, pp. 109–111.
3. See Chapter 11.
4. Dow et al. 1996.
5. Freud 1900, p. 205.
6. Personal observation.

CHAPTER 8: CAR CRASH

1. Kubler-Ross 1969.
2. Freud 1900, pp. 311–546.
3. Freud 1900, p. 392.
4. Pitman and Orr 1990.

CHAPTER 9: JUNKYARD DOG

1. Leroy Brown, song, Jim Croce.
2. This story is told twice in the movie *Colors* (1988) about Los Angeles police officers. The first time Robert Duvall relates it to his junior partner, Sean Penn. The second time Sean Penn repeats it to his junior partner, Sherman Augustus.
3. LaBerge 1985.

CHAPTER 10: HARASSMENT

1. LaBerge 1985.

CHAPTER 11: BRAIN MECHANISMS OF PTSD AND RECOVERY

1. APA DSM-IV, TR 2000.
2. Seligman 1972.
3. van der Kolk 1987; Flannery 1987.
4. Shin et al. 2004, 2005, 2006; Rauch et al. 2006.
5. Damasio 1994; Devinsky et al. 1995; Paus 2001; Rogers et al. 2004.
6. Freud 1933, pp. 71–100.
7. Bajor et al. 2011.
8. Raskind et al. 2003, 2013; Taylor et al. 2008.
9. Delgado et al. 2008; Quirk et al. 2010; Alberini 2011; Graham and Milad 2011; Nader et al. 2013.
10. McGaugh 2004; Nishida et al. 2009.

References

Alberini CM (2011). The role of reconsolidation and the dynamic process of long-term memory formation and storage. *Frontiers in Behavioral Neuroscience* 5:1–10.

American Psychiatric Association (2000). *Diagnostic and Statistical Manual of Mental Disorders*. 4th Edition, Text Revision. Washington, DC: American Psychiatric Press.

Anch AM, Browman CP, Mitler MM, Walsh JK (1988). *Sleep: A Scientific Perspective*. Englewood Cliffs, NJ: Prentice Hall.

Bajor LA, Ticlea AN, Osser DN (2011). The psychopharmacology algorithm project at the Harvard South Shore Program: An Update on Posttraumatic Stress Disorder. *Harv Rev Psychiatry* 19:240–258.

Bettelheim B (1976). *The Uses of Enchantment: The Meaning and Importance of Fairy Tales*. London: Penguin.

Brockway SS (1987). Group treatment of combat nightmares in post-traumatic stress disorder. *J Contemporary Psychotherapy* 17:270–284.

Damasio AR (1994). *Descartes' Error*. New York: G. P. Putnam's Sons.

Davidson JRT, Foa EB (1993). *Posttraumatic Stress Disorder: DSM-IV and Beyond*. Washington DC: American Psychiatric Press.

Delgado MR, Nearing KI, LeDoux JE, Phelps EA (2008). Neural circuitry underlying the regulation of conditioned fear and its relation to extinction. *Neuron* 59:829–838.

Devinsky O, Morrell MJ, Vogt BA (1995). Contributions of anterior cingulate cortex to behavior. *Brain* 118:279–306.

Dow BM (2002). Orientation and color columns in monkey visual cortex. *Cerebral Cortex* 12:1005–1015.

Dow BM, Kelsoe JR, Jr., Gillin JC (1996). Sleep and dreams in Vietnam PTSD and depression. *Biol Psychiatry* 39:42–50.

Flannery RB Jr. (1987). From victim to survivor: A stress management approach in the treatment of learned helplessness. In *Psychological Trauma* (van der Kolk BA, ed.). Washington, DC: American Psychiatric Press, pp. 217–232.

Foa EB, Meadows EA (1997). Psychosocial treatments for posttraumatic stress disorder: A critical review. *Ann Rev Psychol* 48:449–480.

Foa EB, Rothbaum BO (1998). *Treating the Trauma of Rape: Cognitive-behavior Therapy for PTSD*. New York: Guilford.

Forbes D, Phelps AJ, McHugh AF, Debenham P, Hopwood M, Creamer M (2003). Imagery rehearsal in the treatment of posttraumatic nightmares in Australian veterans with chronic combat-related PTSD: 12-month follow-up data. *J Traumatic Stress* 16:509–513.

Freud S (1900). *The Interpretation of Dreams* (Strachey J, trans.). New York: Avon Books.

Freud S (1933). *New Introductory Lectures on Psychoanalysis* (Strachey J, trans.) New York: W.W. Norton & Co.

Hembree EA, Foa EB (2003). Interventions for trauma-related emotional disturbances in adult victims of crime. *J Traumatic Stress* 16:187–199.

Krakow B, Hollifield M, Johnston L, Koss M, Schrader R, Warner TD, Tandberg D, Lauriello J, McBride L, Cutchen L, Cheng D, Emmons S, Germain A, Melendrez D, Sandoval S, Prince H (2001). Imagery rehearsal therapy for chronic nightmares in sexual assault survivors with posttraumatic stress disorder: A randomized controlled trial. *JAMA* 286:537–545.

Kubler-Ross E (1969). *On Death and Dying*. New York: Collier Books.

LaBerge S (1985). *Lucid Dreaming*. New York: Ballantine Books.

McGaugh JL (2004). The amygdala modulates the consolidation of memories of emotionally arousing experiences. *Annu Rev Neurosci* 27:1–28

Moore BA, Krakow B (2007). Imagery rehearsal therapy for acute posttraumatic nightmares among combat soldiers in Iraq. *Am J Psychiatry* 164:683–84.

Nader K, Hardt O, Lanius R (2013). Memory as a new therapeutic target. *Dialogues in Clinical Neuroscience* 15:475–486.

Nishida M, Pearsall J, Buckner RL, Walker MP (2009). REM sleep, prefrontal theta, and the consolidation of human emotional memory 19:1158–1166.

Paus T (2001). Primate anterior cingulate cortex: Where motor control, drive and cognition interface. *Nature Reviews Neuroscience* 2:417–424.

Pitman RK, Orr SP (1990). The black hole of trauma. *Biol Psychiatry* 27: 469–471.

Quirk GJ, Pare D, Richardson R, Herry C, Monfils MH, Schiller D, Vicentic A (2010). Erasing fear memories with extinction training. *J Neurosci* 30:14993–14997.

Raskind MA, Peskind ER, Kanter ED, Petrie EC, Radant A, Thompson CE, Dobie DJ, Hoff D, Rein RJ, Straits-Troster K, Thomas RG, McFall MM (2003).

Reduction of nightmares and other PTSD symptoms in combat veterans by prazosin: A placebo-controlled study. *Am J Psychiatry* 160:371–373.

Raskind MA, Peterson K, Williams T, Hoff DJ, Hart K, Holmes H, Domas D, Hill J, Daniels C, Calohan J, Millard SP, Rohde K, O'Connell J, Pritzl D, Fieszli K, Petrie EC, Gross C, Mayer CL, Freed MC, Engel C, Peskind ER (2013). A trial of prazosin for combat trauma PTSD with nightmares in active-duty soldiers returned from Iraq and Afghanistan. *Am J Psychiatry* 170:1003–1010.

Rauch SL, Shin LM, Phelps EA (2006). Neurocircuitry models of posttraumatic stress disorder and extinction: human neuroimaging research—past, present, and future. *Biol Psychiatry* 60:376–382.

Rogers RD, Ramnani N, Mackay C, Wilson JL, Jezzard P, Carter CS, Smith SM (2004). Distinct portions of anterior cingulate cortex and medial prefrontal cortex are activated by reward processing in separable phases of decision-making cognition. *Biol Psychiatry* 55:594–602.

Seligman ME (1972). Learned helplessness. Ann Rev Med 23:407–12.

Shapiro F (2001). *Eye Movement Desensitization and Reprocessing: Basic Principles,Protocols, and Procedures*. New York: Guilford.

Shapiro F (2013). *Getting Past Your Past*. New York: Rodale.

Shapiro F, Maxfield L (2002). Eye movement sensitization and reprocessing (EMDR): Information processing in the treatment of trauma. *J Clin Psychol* 58:943–946.

Shay J (1994). *Achilles in Vietnam: Combat Trauma and the Undoing of Character*. New York: Simon and Schuster (Touchstone).

Shay J (2002). *Odysseus in America: Combat Trauma and the Trials of Homecoming*. New York: Scribner.

Shin LM, Orr SP, Carson MA, Rauch SL, Macklin ML, Lasko NB, Peters PM, Metzger LJ, Dougherty DD, Cannistraro PA, Alpert NM, Fischman AJ, Pitman RK (2004). Regional cerebral blood flow in the amygdala and medial prefrontal cortex during traumatic imagery in male and female Vietnam veterans with PTSD. *Arch Gen Psychiatry* 61:168–176.

Shin LM, Rauch SL, Pitman RK (2006). Amygdala, medial prefrontal cortex, and hippocampal function in PTSD. *Ann NY Acad Sci* 1071:67–79.

Shin LM, Wright CI, Cannistraro PA, Wedig MM, McMullin K, Martis B, Macklin ML, Lasko NB, Cavanagh SR, Krangel TS, Orr SP, Pitman RK, Whalen PJ, Rauch SL (2005). A functional magnetic resonance imaging study of amygdala and medial prefrontal cortex responses to overtly presented fearful faces in posttraumatic stress disorder. *Arch Gen Psychiatry* 62:273–281.

Taylor FB, Martin P, Thompson C, Williams J, Mellman TA, Gross C, Peskind ER, Raskind MA (2008). Prazosin effects on objective sleep measures and clinical symptoms in civilian trauma PTSD: A placebo-controlled study. *Biol Psychiatry* 63:629–632.

Taylor GJ, Bagby RM, Parker JDA (1997). *Disorders of Affect Regulation: Alexithymia in Medical and Psychiatric Illness*. New York: Cambridge University Press.

van der Kolk BA (1987). The psychological consequences of overwhelming life experiences. In *Psychological Trauma* (van der Kolk BA, ed.). Washington, DC: American Psychiatric Press, pp. 1–30.

Yoshioka T, Dow BM, Vautin RG (1996). Neuronal mechanisms of color categorization in areas V1, V2 and V4 of macaque monkey visual cortex. *Behavioural Brain Research* 76:51–70.

Index

About the Author

Bruce Dow, MD, is a board-certified psychiatrist and psychopharmacologist with more than 20 years of experience in treating posttraumatic stress disorder (PTSD). A past Fulbright Fellow at the University of Strasbourg, he is a 1966 graduate of the University of Rochester School of Medicine. Dow is a Life Fellow of the American Psychiatric Association. He has had two careers, the first in neuroscience (1967–1989), leading to a full professorship at SUNY/Buffalo, the second in clinical psychiatry (1989–present), in Southern California (UC San Diego) and eastern Massachusetts (Vinfen Corporation). His interest in PTSD dates from 1991, when he began working with Vietnam veterans at the San Diego VA Medical Center. He currently provides psychopharmacological treatment in a community setting to patients with serious mental illness.